# Dynamic Christian Fellowship

Dynamic Christian fellowship

by LeRoy Judson Day

Valley Forge
## THE JUDSON PRESS
Chicago                                        Los Angeles

© The Judson Press 1960

Valley Forge, Pa.

Fifth Printing, April, 1962

Cover Design: Sylvia Polis

# Contents

Contents

# Introduction

Three interests have led the author into intensive study of group behavior: one social-scientific, one theological, and one practical. Having been engaged in teaching and research in the fields of sociology and social psychology, he has been stimulated by new understandings of the behavior of people in groups. In the past three decades the social sciences have made tremendous strides in discovering what goes on in groups, what makes groups function well or poorly, and how groups affect the personalities of those who participate in them.

Meanwhile theologians have been busy re-examining the church and have been producing a flood of stimulating writings on the nature and meaning of the church. From the renewed emphasis on the church as an interacting group of people has come new understanding of the significance of the committed fellowship in the experience of the Christian faith and in the development of Christian character and witness.

In addition experiences in the life of churches have created for the author a practical interest in group process. This began early when as a boy he saw his father, a committed Christian layman, take the leadership roles which were needed to make an effective group of a struggling little country church. With little concern for theory but with very effective practice, this dentist-deacon witnessed for Christ in agriculture, education, and in the community. He was a dynamic Christian leader.

Later when the author entered the pastorate, he was called upon to make use of both theoretical and practical knowledge of group life. One congregation was divided by tensions among persons who were no longer able to communicate with one another. Another congregation faced the problem of learning to work together in a major effort to serve the needs of those outside the congregation, and in the world around it.

In this book some of the resulting understandings from social science, theology, and experience are drawn together and applied to the life of the church. The plan of the book is to move from the biblical and theological to the psychological, sociological, and practical. There is no exclusion of one by the other, however, and the reader will need to keep in mind the understanding of divine redemption set forth in the early sections of the book if he is to gain the full significance of later sections.

LeRoy Judson Day

*Alderson Broaddus College*
*Philippi, West Virginia*

6

# I

# Persons, Groups, and Redemption

## A. POWER IN FACE-TO-FACE CHRISTIAN GROUPS

There is power in the Christian fellowship.* There is
power in the face-to-face,** intimate group of people who
share a common commitment to Jesus Christ. This power is
more than the power of numbers. We say that "two heads are
better than one" or that "many hands make light work." We
recognize our collective power as a group when we say that
the group is greater than the individuals who comprise it.
But the power in the Christian fellowship is even greater
than this. The power in the Christian church is the power of
the Holy Spirit. "For where two or three are gathered in my
name, there am I in the midst of them" (Matt. 18:20).

This saying of Jesus, so often quoted to encourage the
faithful when attendance at midweek service is small, is
really one of the profound statements of the New Testament.
The meaning of "there am I in the midst of them" is that
God, through his Holy Spirit, dwells in the group and makes
it a fit vessel for his work. The group ceases to be a collection
of weak and unlovely individuals and through his presence
becomes the church. As the church, the group possesses a
beauty and power which none of its individual members
possess. Collectively its members become the body of Christ
doing his work in the world.

We have only to read the record of the Book of the Acts
of the Apostles to see the effectiveness of this Spirit-filled
fellowship:

"And they devoted themselves to the apostles' teaching
and fellowship, to the breaking of bread and the prayers.

* **CHRISTIAN FELLOWSHIP**—a group of persons bound together by their common
commitment to Christ, united in Christian love and the service of God and their fellow
men.
** **FACE-TO-FACE GROUP**—a group in which every member can see the face of
and respond to the words and actions of every other member.

7

. . . And all who believed were together and had all things in common; . . . And day by day, attending the temple together and breaking bread in their homes, they partook of food with glad and generous hearts, praising God and having favor with all the people. And the Lord added to their number day by day those who were being saved" (Acts 2:42, 44, 46-47).

They were together; they ate together; they prayed together; they shared a common life and worship; and through the winsomeness of their fellowship the Lord worked. The effective power of God is most truly felt in the intimate face-to-face Christian group.

## B. THE PERSON AND THE GROUP

Persons and groups are so closely interconnected that it is impossible to discuss one without the other. Persons make up groups. At the same time, groups influence, shape, and develop persons. From one point of view the character of a group is influenced and controlled by the type of persons who compose it. Each person helps to establish the tone of the group in one way or another. But from the other point of view each personality is at least in part a product of the group. The individual is altered and influenced and even, in a sense, created as a personality by his membership and activity in groups.

Sometimes the study of groups gets halted by an endless argument over which comes first, the group or the individual. For our purposes we need only to recognize the importance of both the person and the group and their significance for each other. We need to remind ourselves that the people who come into contact with church groups have personalities already shaped by previous experience with individuals and groups. The church groups into which they come will be changed by their presence. Nevertheless, since each individual is partly a product of continuing group influences, each personality can be affected and changed by group participation.

## C. WHAT THE GROUP GETS FROM THE PERSON

When adults come into a group, they bring with them a great store of past experiences and influences. John and Mary

8

Thompson, for instance, join the Elm Street Church. They have attitudes, values, and behavior patterns which they have accumulated over the years. The Elm Street Church received with the Thompson's church letters a list of offices they have held and responsibilities they have carried (deacon, choir member, Sunday church school teacher, etc.). This is a help, but it gives only a very inadequate picture of John and Mary as persons. A full picture would have to include such unavailable items as their individual physical and mental characteristics, the groups they have belonged to from birth right up to adulthood, and all the experiences they have had in relation to other persons in and out of those groups.

Sometimes we feel that children are different from adults, that they are still unaffected. But little Mike and Debbie Thompson entering the nursery and kindergarten of the Elm Street Sunday church school are also members of other groups. The family, the play group, and the neighborhood have already influenced their ways of responding to others and their ideas about themselves and their world. The child who doesn't accept the disciplines of the vacation church school kindergarten often is the one whose family indulges his every whim and imposes no disciplines upon him at home. Small children, no less than adults, are separate, distinct, unique persons. Even though Mike and Debbie are brother and sister, they are not the products of exactly identical influences.

Both children and adults bring unique personalities into the group.

## D. WHAT THE PERSON GETS FROM THE GROUP

Let us look at Michael Thompson and see others through him. He is a growing, developing person. He moves progressively through childhood and youth to manhood. He might be thought of as representing any human being. Michael can't be human alone. He is a part of many groups. Not only was he born into a group, the human family, which sustains his physical life, but also he is developing his personality in an environment of groups.

He is learning, and learning comes in social relationships. He learns in the family as mother says, "Don't touch, Michael, the stove is hot." He is becoming acquainted with and learning to use his cultural heritage, that is, the way of life of his society. This, too, comes in the group as he learns and uses language and communication. He understands when a playmate calls out, "Hey, Mike, come over and try my new swing." The same groups from which Michael acquires a cultural heritage also provide him with values and motivations: "You'll have to eat your vegetables if you want to grow up big and strong like Daddy," or "Good boys tell the truth, Michael."

In his group relations, Michael, as he grows and develops, is also acquiring statuses* and roles**; he has a standing in each group and certain behaviors which correspond to his standing. "You may be able to get what you want by yelling when you are playing with the children, but you don't talk like that to your mother, Michael Thompson!" or "That's the way we like to see you behave, Michael; that makes you a good member of the Thompson family."

Like the members of his family, members of other groups in which Michael Thompson participates make evaluations of how well he lives up to their expectations of him. By word or action, in differing ways, all groups let their members know how well they are fulfilling the expected roles and, therefore, how well they are accepted by the group. If Michael's parents consistently call him a "bad boy," Michael will tend to develop a negative impression of himself. If John and Mary frequently refer to him as a "good boy," he may develop quite another estimate of himself.

If Michael's friends consistently exclude him when they are engaged in certain types of activities, he learns that he is not appreciated or wanted. If they consistently include him, his self-regard goes up because he is esteemed by others. It is typical of human beings to be so concerned about having the favorable regard of others that they will even risk life and limb to attain it. How we regard ourselves grows out of how we believe others regard us.

The most important thing a person receives from any and all groups in his life is his own self-acceptance and the related

* STATUS—the position a member has in a group.
** ROLE—the conduct expected by the group of any member in the group, in a particular situation.

10

self-feelings. What he thinks about himself, who he thinks he is, whether or not he is willing to accept himself for what he is, all of these feelings grow out of his group experience. They are the self-feelings that determine behavior, mental health, and even sanity. As a man "thinketh in his heart, so is he" (Prov. 23:7 KJV).

## E. THE GROUP AND SELF-CONCEPTS

Michael Thompson, like every other person, is building a personality out of his relations with others. That personality really takes shape as his sense of selfhood develops. Michael must become conscious of himself as separate and different from other selves.

This self-awareness begins to develop in earliest infancy. An early stage of it is the child's discovery of parts of his own body. He plays with and puts in his mouth a nearby object. Suddenly a bite brings the discovery that a finger is a part of him. He discovers that this body is his.

The developing concept of the self, however, is an even greater discovery than this. Each experience we pass through in relation to others as we grow to manhood and womanhood gives us impressions of ourselves. Gradually through childhood, youth, and adulthood we get a picture, a mental image, of what we are. This self-image is the most distinctively human part of us.

We can use the first person pronouns (I, me, mine) meaningfully because of this reflexive self, this picture of self that is reflected back to us. It is our relations with other people that make it possible for us to have attitudes toward ourselves. Michael Thompson can be both subject and object at the same time and say, "I hurt myself." Even more significantly, he can later in life evaluate his own behavior in terms of his own conception of himself and say, "I was ashamed of myself," or "I was proud of myself," or "I am not myself today."

## F. TOGETHERNESS, SEPARATENESS, AND LOSTNESS

This very self-consciousness which is basic to our human personality is also our undoing. While self-awareness springs from our relationships with others, that same self-awareness

11

is ultimately destructive of those very relationships. All of us tend to become enamored of self. We turn self-conscious in the extreme and are so wrapped up in ourselves that we become unpleasant, unsatisfactory, and even impossible persons to have around, almost forcing others to abandon their relationships with us. When this happens, the self developed in social contacts is left isolated, cut off from the very interactions with persons and groups that brought it into being. It is possible to be totally selfish; but what an impossible kind of life that creates!

Human personality is created in the image of God. "So God created man in his own image, in the image of God he created him; male and female he created them" (Gen. 1:27). That is, God made us persons as he is a Person, able to communicate with other persons and to live in fellowship with them. He made us capable of togetherness.* This is not the physical "togetherness" achieved by the college students who tried to see how many people they could crowd into one telephone booth. The togetherness of which God has made us capable is the interaction of persons in mutuality.** We can share one another's concerns.

Linked with this capacity for mutuality and togetherness, however, is the basic human pitfall of selfishness and self-centeredness, as we have seen this demonstrated in Michael Thompson. Michael can say "we" with real feeling, for he is a part of others and they are a part of him; but, at the same time, he wants to be himself. "I can do it myself" is his vehement response as a child when help is offered. He wants to be self-reliant. Likewise, as an adult he wants to express his own will, to determine his own destiny. It is in this very self-assertion, this extreme self-centeredness, that Michael abandons the real togetherness for which God created him and which is so essential to him. He abandons it before he has fully attained it. In his selfishness he is lost. His self-centeredness is a denial of his own essential humanity and thus a denial of the Creator in whose image he is made.

This is the legacy of sin to which man in his human weakness is heir. He offends himself, his fellows, and his Creator.

* **TOGETHERNESS**—the sharing in the deepest sense of common interests, concerns, and activities; living and working together as a team.
** **MUTUALITY**—the sharing of each other's interests, concerns, and needs.

12

"Thou hast made him little less than God, and dost crown him with glory and honor . . . thou hast put all things under his feet" (Ps. 8:5-6).

But instead of fulfilling this destiny, man in his self-centeredness chooses to live as less than human. Instead of having everything "under his feet," he becomes the slave to things and to self. He lives like a beast, a plant, or a stone. He permits the beastly to dominate in him by giving himself to selfish passion. He draws from his surroundings all that he can and gives nothing back. He even becomes content with mere existence. When this happens, he is lost. The living soul God breathed into him at creation dies in isolation. The wages of the sin of self-centeredness is the death of the human spirit.

Thus man becomes a lost soul. To abandon togetherness for separateness* is self-destructive. The very self that seeks to assert itself is damaged and ultimately destroyed. To be a real person, one must be able to accept himself, and self-acceptance comes through being accepted in relations with others. No person can exist in complete isolation. Only in relations with others can his life have sufficient meaning to nourish his sanity.

The ultimate relationship which gives meaning and life to the person is his relationship with the divine Self, the great Person, the Creator. Sin is the self assertion that separates man from God. "I am the master of my fate, I am the captain of my soul," he shouts to his Creator—thereby committing the sin that destroys him. In spite of his defiant shout, man finds himself master of nothing and captain of nothing. He is but a slave to the selfishness which consumes him. In his lost state he can only cry out again and again, "Woe is me, for I am lost. . . . Father, I have sinned. . . . Do you not care if we perish?"

From such a lost state man needs to be redeemed. He needs to become a new creature in Christ Jesus. He needs to have the image of God restored. He needs to gain a togetherness which is not centered in self. He needs to gain a togetherness which does not contain the seeds of its own destruction.

* **SEPARATENESS**—the overemphasis of one's individuality to the exclusion of other people; going it alone as a "lone wolf."

13

# G. REDEMPTION*—RESTORED RELATIONSHIPS

We have seen that it was in relationships with others that Michael Thompson gained a sense of self and thus became a person. It was also in relationships that his self-conception was damaged, the image of God was denied, and Michael Thompson became estranged from God and his fellow men. Like others, he was unable to reconcile his separateness with his togetherness and became a lost soul. It follows, therefore, that if he is to be redeemed, if the image of God is to be restored and his human nature re-created, this also will have to occur in relationships.

The basic problem for all mankind is one of reconciliation. Having, in self-centeredness, destroyed his relationships with God and his fellow man, man needs to have those relationships restored. The essential relationship is the one with his Creator. If this is restored, the relationships with his fellow creatures may then also be re-established.

The ministry of reconciliation by which these relationships are restored is the work of Christ. This is no easy task. It costs in terms of real suffering and is characterized by compassion and love — the redemptive love that led to the cross on Calvary.

"Remember that you were at that time separated from Christ, . . . having no hope and without God in the world. But now in Christ Jesus you who once were far off have been brought near in the blood of Christ. For he is our peace, who has made us both one, and has broken down the dividing wall of hostility, by abolishing in his flesh the law of commandments and ordinances, that he might create in himself one new man in place of the two, so making peace, and might reconcile us both to God in one body through the cross, thereby bringing the hostility to an end. . . . So then you are no longer strangers and sojourners, but you are fellow citizens with the saints and members of the household of God" (Eph. 2:12-16, 19).

"And you, who once were estranged and hostile in mind, doing evil deeds, he has now reconciled in his body of

---

* REDEMPTION—salvation from sin and the restoration of the relationship with God which had been broken by sin. Redemption is accomplished by the action of God, particularly through his self-disclosure in the life, death, and resurrection of Jesus Christ, and by the response of the individual to God's redemptive action.

14

flesh by his death, in order to present you holy and blameless and irreproachable before him" (Col. 1:21-22).

God in compassion and love seeks to redeem Michael Thompson and all other lost and isolated souls. He reaches out to the lost through human groups. The redemptive love of God is made known through Christian fellowship. The church as a fellowship of faith is a "colony of heaven" which witnesses to the love of God in Christ. Jesus said, "You shall be my witnesses," and through the church Michael may catch a glimpse of the relationship that can be. He is a prodigal son who, seeing the fellowship of those living in communion with the heavenly Father, may yearn for the re-establishment of the lost relationship.

"This is eternal life, that they know thee the only true God, and Jesus Christ whom thou hast sent" (John 17:3). The ultimate need of each one is the divine society, the very relationship of mutuality with God which the sin of self destroys. The basic problem of mankind is the need for this reconciliation.

## H. COMMITMENT—THE DENYING OF SELF

For Michael Thompson, whose self-centeredness and self-will block the way to fellowship with his Creator, the only hope is to be freed from bondage to self. Christ calls him to deny himself. He is not to deny himself something, but to deny himself, to dethrone self and place God at the center of his life. When Jesus said, "If any man would come after me, let him deny himself and take up his cross and follow me" (Mark 8:34), he was talking about this total commitment which is the only answer to the selfishness which is sin.

Self must abdicate the throne on which Michael Thompson has placed it. Instead, Michael must enthrone Christ as the Lord of his life and Master of his soul. He must be willing to lose himself in devotion to God and his neighbor. "For whoever would save his life will lose it; and whoever loses his life for my sake, he will save it" (Luke 9:24). Michael's salvation from the sin of self will have come when he can say with Paul, "It is no longer I who live, but Christ who lives in me" (Gal. 2:20).

# I. REDEEMED PERSONS IN CHRISTIAN GROUPS

If we are to experience and avail ourselves of the power of God in face-to-face Christian groups, we need to understand something of the nature of the persons who make up those groups and come into contact with them. It is for this purpose that we have reviewed the group experience of Michael Thompson. We have observed how his personality took shape in relations with others. We have noted that his developing self-conception is, at one and the same time, the strength of his personality and his fatal weakness. We have seen him lost in his self-centeredness and then restored to relationship through the redemptive love of God. His redemption, made effective by total commitment, we have recognized to be a social experience linking him with God and with the fellowship of the church, and bringing him into a new relationship with all humanity. We turn now to the question of what the church is and how it functions as a group.

## Questions for Discussion

1. In what ways does a group influence the persons who belong to it?
2. In what ways does a person influence the group to which he belongs?
3. How does a person's attitude toward himself affect his behavior toward others?
4. What does it mean to deny oneself?
5. Why does "joining God" also join us to other Christians?
6. In what ways is your group within the church a redemptive fellowship?

## Suggested Reading

*The Gift of Power,* Lewis Joseph Sherrill, Macmillan, New York, 1955.

The first three chapters of this book provide a fuller discussion of "The Human Self," "Threats to the Self," and "The Christian Community."

*The Church Redemptive,* Howard Grimes, Abingdon Press, Nashville, 1958.

While the reader will find the entire book stimulating, portions of Chapter II relate especially to the present theme.

*Faith, Freedom and Selfhood,* Charles R. Stinette, Jr., The Seabury Press, Greenwich, 1959.

This "study in personal dynamics" by a man well versed in psychiatry and religion, sees the regaining of personhood through community as our greatest need.

*Herein Is Love,* Reuel L. Howe, Judson Press, Valley Forge, Pa., 1961.

*Social Psychology,* Solomon Asch, Prentice-Hall, New York, 1952. Chapter 10.

*Social Psychology,* Alfred Lindesmith and Anselm Strauss, Dryden Press, New York, 1956. Chapters 12 and 13.

## II

# The Redemptive Purpose of the Church

## A. THE CHURCH AND REDEMPTION

The church is the group through which God works in a
unique way to bring his redemption to persons. It is his
agency. He has given it a special mission to carry out for
him. God reaches out to the lost through the church. His
redeeming love is made known through the church. The
church is the fellowship of faith which witnesses to the love
of God and his saving power.

Each one of us is lost in selfishness and sin and needs the
ministries of the church. First, *we need a herald of salvation.*
How else will we hear what God has done for his lost creation? We need to see the joy of fellowship with God and
with one another, which is available to those who have experienced the redemption God has wrought.

Second, *we need the ministry of the church for Christian
nurture.* As self-centered persons we are released from the
living death of slavery-to-self as we accept the grace and love
of God as revealed in Jesus Christ and in grateful response
commit our whole being to God. We become "new creatures
in Christ Jesus," and as new creatures need new personalities.
The old ways have been rejected, but the new ways of the
dedicated life have to be established. This involves more
than simply learning the ideas and values of the new life. It
involves learning to live together in the Christian fellowship;
and this takes place in the group, the church group.

Third, *we need the ministry of Christian service.* If the
new life of dedication to Christ is to be a real escape from
the bondage to self, it must find means of expression. The
church provides avenues for such expression. The self-
forgetting love of the Christian for all of God's creation moves

18

us to action. In the church we find challenges to Christian service and opportunities for joint service with others.

## B. NEW TESTAMENT PICTURES OF THE CHURCH

The New Testament writers did not define the church. They were more concerned with being the church. What they tell us about the essence of the church is given in a number of pictures of the church. Each of these pictures or concepts adds to our understanding because it comes with a different force and draws a different sketch of the relationships involved. Many Christian scholars feel that the most graphic and meaningful of these pictures are: "the people of God," "the body of Christ," and "the fellowship of the Holy Spirit."

### 1. The People of God

The social or group character of the church is evident in the understanding of the church as the people of God. We so easily fall into the error of speaking or thinking of the church as a building, an organization, or an institution. All too often, also, we think of God's means of telling the story of salvation to all the world as being a book, or a code, or a ritual. But both ideas are wrong. The church Christ left behind and the witness God has chosen for himself are a people, the people of God. This is clearly seen in New Testament descriptions of the early Christians.

"I will be their God, and they shall be my people" (2 Cor. 6:16).

"But you are a chosen race, a royal priesthood, a holy nation, God's own people, that you may declare the wonderful deeds of him who called you out of darkness into his marvelous light. Once you were no people but now you are God's people; once you had not received mercy but now you have received mercy" (1 Pet. 2:9-10).

When the people of God are spoken of as a "chosen race," some might be misled to thinking they are chosen for special favors. This is certainly not the case. The evidence is clear from the Scriptures that they are chosen for witnessing, not for favors.

This concept also calls to attention other characteristics of the people of God. They become his people not by natural birth but by a summons. God calls them. These ordinary people become God's people not by the way they are organized or recruited, but by God's action and their personal commitment — their faithfulness and obedience to God and their willingness to be used by him. They are a unity; not many peoples, but one people. Robert Handy in his book, *Members One of Another,* points out

> "that the local congregations are part of the whole church on earth, and that the whole church is nothing without its specific manifestations. . . . the church exists only where particular people have responded concretely to God's call."[1]

The church is the people of God, a community summoned to live as his people. By its very existence and by its life the church declares the marvelous works of God in breaking the power of sin and death and freeing men to walk in newness of life.

## 2. The Body of Christ

Though the New Testament emphasizes the unity of the people of God, we still tend to think of the church as simply a gathering of people. Therefore we need the picture of the church as the body of Christ. We are not just a collection of people, but the people of God. We are not just a body of members, but the body of Christ.

In the New Testament, and especially in the writings of Paul, the term "body" is not equivalent to a corpse, that is, flesh without personality. A body is a living totality functioning through all its parts. Every aspect of feeling, emotion, and thought is described as localized in one or another part of the body. The expression "the body," therefore, is equivalent to the total person, involving the physical, mental, and spiritual aspects of his life. Thus the picture of the church as the body of Christ makes it clear that the church and Christ are inseparable. Christ is the head of the church. The church is subject to him. He dwells in the world in his church. Paul says:

> "Now you are the body of Christ and individually members of it" (1 Cor. 12:27).

[1] Robert T. Handy, *Members One of Another,* The Judson Press, 1959, p. 64.

20

"So we, though many, are one body in Christ, and individually members one of another" (Rom. 12:5).

"For just as the body is one and has many members, and all the members of the body, though many, are one body, so it is with Christ. For by one Spirit we were all baptized into one body — Jews or Greeks, slaves or free — and all were made to drink of one Spirit" (1 Cor. 12:12-13).

The body of Christ is a living organism. As such it has all the dynamic aspects of living things. It does not remain static. It has life and power. It is not bound to rigid form. It grows, changes, and is renewed. But all of this is within the bounds of its faithfulness to Christ, its head. The church is not subservient to political changes or to national culture, for it is Christ's. It is his body.

## 3. The Fellowship of the Holy Spirit

This picture of the church is especially useful for the study of the group life of the church. Togetherness is inherent in the church. Christians experience a most compelling kinship. They owe their redemption to a common Savior. The very fact of their common commitment to Christ and the new life they have in him draws them together.

The fellowship of the Spirit is not a superficial fellowship. It is far deeper than the sociability we associate with the fellowship hall or the fellowship supper. Christians do not *have* fellowship, they *are* a fellowship. Theirs is a real comradeship, a brotherhood. The Christian life creates a new community* — not in the geographic or sociological sense, but in the sense of having solidarity and participating together in activities, values, goals, and a faith which are held in common.

The New Testament writers speak of this togetherness as a *koinonia* which means a possessing-in-common, a sharing, a fellowship, a partnership, a participating-together. The phrase translated "the communion of the saints" refers not just to partaking of the Lord's Supper, but to the participating-together in many things and the deep interpersonal** relations within the church. Nor is the interpersonal sharing within the church limited to human persons. God, the divine

* COMMUNITY—a body of persons having common interests, principles, or concerns and possessing a sense of sharing something which is vital and which knits them together as a group.

** INTERPERSONAL—pertaining to activity or conversation among persons.

21

Person, is there in the fellowship. That is what makes it the church and not just another organization. The Holy Spirit is God himself at work among us. It is the presence of the Holy Spirit that gives power and unity to the church. This presence is a miracle akin to the miracle of the incarnation and the resurrection. God participates together with men and women in the church.

It is not just coincidence that the second chapter of Acts, which tells the story of the gift of the Holy Spirit to the followers of Christ gathered in Jerusalem at Pentecost, is also the chapter which emphasizes again and again the togetherness of Christians.

"And they devoted themselves to the apostles' teaching and *fellowship*, to the breaking of bread and the prayers. . . . And all who believed were together and had all things in common; . . . And day by day, attending the temple *together* and breaking bread in their homes, they partook of food with glad and generous hearts (A.V. 'singleness of heart'), praising God and having favor with all the people. And the Lord added to their number day by day those who were being saved" (Acts 2:42, 44, 46-47).

Even Jews and Greeks, bondsmen and free, male and female were brought together by the power of the Spirit, the New Testament record tells us. Paul writes of them as being "knit together in love" (Col. 2:2). In our own times, too, the Holy Spirit creates real fellowship among people of diverse racial, cultural, and social backgrounds. The unity among them is not so much organizational or creedal as it is deeply spiritual. It is because of this spiritual nature of the fellowship that the church exists not only when the people of God are physically together. Nor does the togetherness of Christians take place only in church buildings and church services. Whether gathered in one place to devote themselves "to the apostles' teaching and fellowship, to the breaking of bread and the prayers," or dispersed in the world carrying out through their daily occupations the calling of God to be his witness in a world which has not accepted the salvation wrought in Christ, Christians are still the fellowship of the Holy Spirit.

Much has been made among some Christian groups of the individual experience of the Holy Spirit — so much, in fact,

22

that they have obscured the truth that the Holy Spirit in the New Testament church was given and experienced in the fellowship of committed persons. Lesslie Newbigin clarifies this idea:

"The Holy Spirit is now no more an occasional visitant to a favored individual, but the abiding and indwelling principle of life in a fellowship. . . . Life in the Spirit is precisely life in the one body of Christ, wherein there is no room at the center for 'I' or 'we,' but He is all in all."[2]

The theologian, Emil Brunner, expresses the idea even more strongly when he writes:

"Where the Holy Ghost is, there is the Christian communion. And the Holy Ghost is not otherwise there than as the Spirit given to the community."[3]

In this way the group of committed persons takes on added significance. It is in the church that the Spirit dwells. The church is the fellowship of the Holy Spirit, not because individuals who have experienced the Spirit have fellowship in the church, but because the Spirit is experienced in and through the group. This is what makes the church such a different kind of fellowship from all other fellowships and organizations.

It is in such a fellowship that the Christian shares. He belongs to the church, a divine community in which Christ dwells through his Spirit. In the church each of us belongs to the people of God, Christ's body, chosen and gathered by him for the special task of witnessing in the world to the love and grace and mercy of God.

## C. THE REDEMPTIVE CHURCH

Redemption is an act of God. Redeemed man is freed from slavery to sin and self and is restored to wholeness of life, peace within himself, and communion with God. This is accomplished by the act of God in Jesus Christ.

When we call the church redemptive,* we do not mean that the church does the redeeming. God alone can do that. But the church is redemptive in another sense of the word.

[2] Lesslie Newbigin, *The Household of God*, Friendship Press, 1954, pp. 115-116. Used by permission.

[3] From *The Misunderstanding of the Church*, by Emil Brunner, Copyright, 1953, by W. L. Jenkins, The Westminster Press, p. 11. Used by permission.

* REDEMPTIVE—that which aids in achieving the purposes of redemption, or which helps the individual to be aware of and respond to God's redemptive action.

It is related to redemption. The redeeming act of God in Christ gathers us into his church; but the church brings the message of redemption to the world. The Master told those he left behind:

"You shall receive power when the Holy Spirit has come upon you; and *you shall be my witnesses* in Jerusalem and in all Judea and Samaria and to the end of the earth" (Acts 1:8).

It is apparent that our Lord had no other plan for the evangelization of the world. When, therefore, it is asked, "Can an individual be saved apart from the church?" the answer is, No. The gospel has to be communicated before man can hear it and experience God's redemption; and since the church has been the witness God has used for this communication, man cannot be saved apart from the church. From apostolic eyewitnesses down to the present day the church has made known the good news of redemption. When it has failed to witness, it has failed to be the church.

## 1. The Witness of the Church

The function of the church is to "declare the wonderful deeds of him who called you out of darkness into his marvelous light" (1 Pet. 2:9) and to proclaim the good news, the gospel of Jesus Christ. It is for this that God has chosen his people, the church.

"Evangelism, therefore is not a more or less necessary invention, contrivance, or decision of man . . . . a chosen man of God is not even free to ponder or to decide whether or not he will take up or continue day by day the mission for which he is chosen."[4]

The church is to witness.

This witnessing is a *vocal* function. The church must speak the Word of God and tell the story of the redeeming love of God. It does this in many ways: in simple language and in eloquent sermon; on the printed page and through mass media such as radio and television; through the appeal of the evangelist and through the personal testimony of the faithful.

It is a *dramatic* function, also. The life, death, and resur-

[4] Markus Barth, *The Broken Wall*, The Judson Press, 1959, p. 173.

rection of Christ and the rebirth of the human soul are portrayed again and again wherever the church meets in worship. This is especially true of baptism and the Lord's Supper, but it is also true of every act of worship.

Witnessing is more, however. If words are to ring true and symbolic acts are to have meaning, the church — the people of God, the fellowship of redeemed persons — must be an exhibit of redemption to the world. In other words, witnessing is also a *life* function. Actions speak louder than words. A first century pagan said, "Behold these Christians how they love one another." Paul, the apostle, said that one might "speak in the tongues of men and of angels" and yet miss the "still more excellent way," the way of self-forgetting love. Thus the life of the Christian and of the redeemed fellowship becomes the primary way of carrying out the function of witnessing.

It is the life of the Christian group that gives significance to the testimony of words. How Christians feel and behave toward one another and toward the world is crucial to the successful reception of their message.

The blood of the martyrs was the seed of the church because the behavior of the martyrs was clear evidence of transformed lives. Their courage, their faith, their love for those of the world as well as those of their own fellowship were eloquent. If the life of the church today does not witness to the power of God to transform selfish, sin-ridden humanity, then all other efforts to evangelize are of no avail. The deportment of the church and of the individual Christian whose life the church nurtures is of the utmost importance.

The good news to which each individual bears witness is the message of the community, that is, the church. It is not just his own message.

"The normal process by which the gospel is made known is for one person who has been touched by the community of persons whose lives have been transformed by the gospel to reach out to another person and draw him into the Christian community. This process is in keeping with the way the human self emerges in the first place."[5]

Every member is a witness. The Reformation doctrine of the

[5] Howard Grimes, *The Church Redemptive*, Abingdon Press, 1958, p. 27. Used by permission.

priesthood of the believers means not only that each man is his own priest having direct access to God, but also that each Christian is a priest for others. He has a redemptive responsibility. He is a priest unto whom God has entrusted the "ministry of reconciliation." The redemptive church is a witnessing church.

## 2. The Nurture of the Church

The redemptive task of the church does not end with the proclamation of the gospel and the response of the sinner to the call of God. There is a task of Christian nurture to be performed. The "new creature in Christ Jesus" has a new orientation, a new life center. But he does not automatically acquire a new personality. One whose whole personality has been self-centered must develop a new Christ-centered personality. He has to fight against the old ways, for they have become habits with him. But the committed life is not transformed by its own power; "God is at work in you, both to will and to work for his good pleasure" (Phil. 2:13).

Just as in infancy the individual began growing a self-centered personality, so as a "babe in Christ" he grows a Christ-centered personality. This does not happen all at once. Human personality is built in relationships with others in the home, the neighborhood, the school, in the play group, and in all the other groups in which a person is involved. The Christian personality of the "new creature in Christ Jesus" is developed also in relationship with others in groups. The Christian home and other Christ-infused groups play their part; but the key group for the development of Christian personality is the church. Therefore, Christian nurture is a vital part of the church's redemptive task.

## 3. The Service of the Church

It is no mere coincidence that Christian people are leaders in the field of service to their fellow men. Since God so loved the world that he gave his Son, the people of God must also care for the world. Their concern is expressed not only in witnessing, but also in outgoing Christian service. The compassion of Christ is exemplified by the church. Wherever there is suffering, pain, or need of any kind, Christian people will be found serving that need. Christian charity, hospitals, medical and agricultural missions, disaster relief, and countless other examples could be cited. These are true responses to the command given in the Great Commission to "go therefore and make disciples of all nations" (Matt. 28:19).

But Christian acts of service can never be thought of as a sort of "bait" to catch converts. Anything of that sort is less than Christian. Ventures in Christian service come out of the overflowing heart of love, without ulterior motives. The selflessness of the committed life is expressed in deeds of mercy, loving-kindness, and benevolence to all men by individual Christians and the Christian group.

"Come, O blessed of my Father, . . . for I was hungry and you gave me food, I was thirsty and you gave me drink, I was a stranger and you welcomed me, I was naked and you clothed me, I was sick and you visited me, I was in prison and you came to me. . . . as you did it to one of the least of these my brethren, you did it to me" (Matt. 25:34-36, 40).

Like the good Samaritan, each individual Christian can and must serve his neighbor when and where the need arises, without thought of gain. The church, too, as a group is in the world to serve, also without thought of gain. The challenge to Christian service and the provision of channels for acts of service is an important function of the church and a part of its redemptive task.

## D. THE GROUP ASPECT OF THE CHURCH

### 1. *The Local Church*

The church, we have said, is the people of God, the body of Christ, the dwelling place of the Holy Spirit. It is the witness of God, the instrument for Christian nurture, the challenge to Christ-like service. But somehow this does not all correspond to the local church as we experience it. "Surely he can't be talking about the church I belong to. Old Main Street Church was never like this." No, and neither is Crane Creek Church out in the country, nor Prospect Park Church in the new housing development. No local church is totally and fully the church as Christ intended it.

27

"She (the church) is not a perfect assembly, but an on-going fellowship for growing and gathering. She lives always 'in the process of formation.' "[6]

To be a Christian means to be in the company of God's people, the church. To belong to the church means to be a member of a particular congregation in a particular tradition with all the impediments and frailties to which human institutions and individuals are subject.

Some of the failure of the local church stems from the fact that not all of its members are committed persons. People have been known to join a church simply as a social organization, like they would join a club. Some of the failure of the local church stems also from the fact that even committed members are not fully perfected. Awareness of the failures and imperfections of the churches has led some people to attempt to bypass the church, to be Christians without becoming a part of a church. If we were to ignore for the moment the historic role of the church in preserving the Scriptures and in witnessing to the revelation of God in Christ, we might admit that an individual could experience redemption apart from a local church. But as Elton Trueblood has pointed out,

"The moment we really feel the touch of Christ's hand upon us, we are forced to start supporting or producing the kind of fellowship which alone can extend His ministry in contemporary experience."[7]

"To enter into communion with one's fellow Christians is to enter most immediately and inescapably into that visual community, the local congregation. To come to terms with the church is to come to terms with it in its most concrete form — the local company of Christ's people gathered together in church order."[8]

The commitment of the Christian to Christ involves a commitment to his fellow Christians, said Martin Luther. A church is a covenant community. Not only have a number of people covenanted with God; they have also covenanted with one another. In a particular local situation and within

[6] Markus Barth, *op. cit.*, p. 107.

[7] D. Elton Trueblood, *Finding God in the Redemptive Fellowship*, The Upper Room, 1958, p. 13. Used by permission.

[8] From an unpublished manuscript by Harry Kruener, Howard Moody, and Harvey Cox. Used by permission.

the traditions of a common culture, they have associated in a group supporting and producing the local Christian fellowship. John Wesley defined the local church as "a company of men having the form and seeking the power of godliness, united in order to pray together, to receive the word of exhortation and to watch over one another in love."[9] (We would add, to witness to the world the love and grace of God toward all men.) We experience the reality of being God's people in the local gathered community* of those who have responded to God's call and have covenanted themselves together as the community of God's people. The local church is the manifestation in the local community of the people of God.

Obviously that manifestation will be something less than perfect. We have observed that not all the members of the local congregation will at all times be fully in accord with the Holy Spirit in all aspects of thought and behavior. And just as individuals may vary from time to time, so also may the local church be nearer at times to the will of its Master than at other times. This gap, between what we are as a local church and what Christ would have us to be, we are constantly trying to close. Knowing our human limitations, we may never expect to fully close it. Nonetheless, we would be failing in our commitment if we did not try to reduce it to a minimum. In fact, the closing of this gap is one of the concerns of this present study.

## 2. The Church as a Group

One important aspect of the church is that it is a group. The local manifestation of the people of God, the body of Christ, the fellowship of the Holy Spirit is a human group. It is a group because it is composed of interacting personalities. It is a number of people in reciprocal communication — how many people and how effective the communication between them will depend upon the church, the life of its members, the frequency and nature of its meetings, and many other factors.

[9] Howard Grimes, *op. cit.*, p. 34. Used by permission.

* GATHERED COMMUNITY—this phrase is used to characterize the Christian church which was gathered or constituted as a special group by God for the achievement of a particular purpose. A Greek word in the New Testament, *ekklesia*, is translated "church" and means literally "called out." Thus the church is thought of as a community of persons who have been called out by God and provided with a special life and mission.

29

Frequently local churches have wondered about their size and the danger of their getting too large for the maintenance of fellowship. An early group of Protestants included the following article in their "Declaration of Faith":

"That the members off everie Church or Congregacion ought to knowe one another, that so they may performe all the duties off love one towards another both to soule and bodie. Mat. 18.15. I Thes. 5.14. I Cor. 12.25. And especiallie the Elders ought to knowe the whole flock, whereoff the HOLIE GHOST hath made them overseers. Acts 20.28; I Pet. 5.2,3. And therefore a Church ought not to consist off such a multitude as cannot have particuler knowledg one off another." [10]

The members of one church may see each other for an extended period on Sunday, during which there is real participation in and sharing of a common faith and their mutual experiences of it. They may also be in contact with each other during the week and share numerous aspects of their common life. In contrast, the members of another church may see each other for only an hour or two on Sunday morning. During that time most of the communication may be of a formal one-way variety, that is, one person lecturing to a Sunday church school class, or the minister preaching to the congregation. Beyond this, their paths may rarely if ever cross during the week, and they may have no life experiences in common except as they share in the services of the church.

This second sort of church can hardly be called a group. It may, however, have or develop a number of small groups within itself and do this so effectively that it becomes, in fact, a cluster of groups. In such a case, it must be remembered that "its numerous fellowship, study, and service units — are just as essentially 'the church' as are its larger corporate meetings." [11] We might add that these numerous groups are probably much more effective in changing lives than the larger corporate meetings. Still, some churches may be small enough in numbers, direct and personal enough in inter-

[10] W. J. McGlothlin, "A Declaration of Faith of English People Remaining at Amsterdam in Holland" (1611) in *Baptist Confessions of Faith,* American Baptist Publication Society, 1911, p. 90.

[11] Harry C. Munro, *Fellowship Evangelism through Church Groups,* The Bethany Press, 1951, p. 23. Used by permission.

action, and have frequent enough contacts among their members to be literally single groups.

A group is more than a collection of individuals, though individuals make it up. A church is more than just a gathering of Christians. S. R. Slavson has defined a group as consisting of

> "three or more persons in an informal relation where there is a maximum interpenetration* and prolonged direct emotional activity among the individuals constituting it, and as a result of which the personality of each member is modified."[12]

The redemptive church has the goal of "changed" persons, of helping people become new persons in Christ. If it is to fulfill its redemptive purpose, however, it will need to be the sort of group in which the "maximum interpenetration and prolonged direct emotional activity among the individuals constituting it" is achieved.

"Changed" persons might be achieved in other ways. Commanding certain types of behavior and forbidding others might change persons, at least in their outer conduct. Persons might be changed by the coercive intervention of the persons, at least in their outer conduct. Persons might be changed by the coercive intervention of the Deity. But God has chosen to give man freedom, freedom to grow and to develop. Man grows, develops, and is changed in his association with others. Therefore,

> "The commandment to love God, and our neighbor as ourselves, is taken here to be not so much a responsibility laid upon us as a description of our deepest spiritual need."[13]

We need the redeeming power of the relationship with God which we can have in Christ and which is mediated to us through the Holy Spirit in the church group.

Any church which is seeking to accomplish its redemptive mission must be more than an aggregate of individuals. It must be a dynamic group. It must provide for direct and

* INTERPENETRATION—indicates the flow of ideas and feelings among two or more persons in which there is a depth of mutual understanding.

[12] S. R. Slavson, "The Dynamics of Group Process," reprinted from *Character Education in a Democracy*, Chap. IV, in *Readings in Group Work*, ed. Dorothea F. Sullivan, Association Press, 1952, p. 223. Used by permission.

[13] John L. Casteel, *Spiritual Renewal through Personal Groups*, Association Press, 19′ p. 19. Used by permission.

frequent interaction among its members; and this interaction must not be of a formal impersonal sort nor consist of mere surface sociability. It must encourage maximum interpenetration of personalities. Only then will the central Person of the church be truly known, and only then will the full redemptive power of God be applied to the individual life.

## Questions for Discussion

1. Why do Christians experience "a most compelling kinship?"

2. If it is God who redeems, how can a church be redemptive?

3. Why does every Christian need the church?

4. How can the term redemption be applied to Christian nurture?

5. How can the term redemption be applied to the service function of the church?

6. When does your church group act out of love and compassion "without ulterior motives"?

7. How can you increase the "interaction" and "interpenetration" that will make your local church more of a group?

## Suggested Reading

*Spiritual Renewal through Personal Groups,* John L. Casteel, Association Press, New York, 1957.

This is a description of actual experiences in personal groups in local churches and how they helped to change persons.

*The Church Redemptive,* Howard Grimes, Abingdon Press, Nashville, 1958.

Especially Chapter IV on "The Fellowship of the Spirit" is pertinent.

*Finding God in the Redemptive Fellowship,* D. Elton Trueblood, The Upper Room, Nashville, 1958.

This thirty-page pamphlet relates as much to the family as to the church, viewing both as redemptive fellowships.

# III

# The Group Life of the Church

The church is, in one of its most important aspects, a group. It is a group because a church is a number of people in reciprocal, or two-way, communication. It is a group also because the members of a church recognize their mutuality and togetherness. They identify themselves with their fellows in their frequent use of statements which include the word "we." But the church is a group in an even deeper sense. Group behavior is of the very nature of the church and the Christian commitment. The church is the community of the Holy Spirit.

## A. THE COMMUNITY OF THE SPIRIT

God has created a new community in the world, a community actualized in many local situations. Its group character is emphasized again and again in the New Testament where it is referred to as "the people of God," "the household of faith," "the fellowship of the Holy Spirit." This new community of the Spirit came into being at Pentecost when the Holy Spirit came upon the committed group. It exists as a community not for its own sake but for the redemptive purpose of God.

In the words of Suzanne De Dietrich, the community is "both the instrument and the token of God's saving purpose."[1] It is the instrument in that its task is proclaiming the gospel. "You shall be my witnesses" (Acts 1:8). Insofar as it is the embodiment of the rule of God, it is the token that the redemption promised by God is an accomplished fact. The presence of the Holy Spirit attests to this. The group and the presence of the Holy Spirit in the group are both

[1] From *The Witnessing Community*, by Suzanne De Dietrich, Copyright, 1958, by W. L. Jenkins, The Westminster Press, p. 146. Used by permission.

essential aspects of the church. They come together; not in sequence.

"One does not first believe and then join in the fellowship: but one becomes a believer just because one shares in the gift vouchsafed to the fellowship."[2]

The Acts of the Apostles makes it clear that doing things together characterized the early Jerusalem church. In his epistles, Paul reminded the young churches of Asia and Greece of their need for love, sharing, and understanding. This emphasis upon togetherness was made not simply because it was good for Christians to participate together. It was made because without togetherness there is no people of God, no witnessing community of the Spirit, no self-transcending community to mediate the redemption of God to the world.

Group life is of the very nature of the church because of the nature of Christian commitment. Freedom from bondage to sin and self comes through self-denial, in the dethroning of self through the commitment to love and serve God. This establishes the vertical relationship between man and God. But there must also be a horizontal relationship between man and his neighbor. One cannot offer true worship to God when he has anything against his brother (Matt. 5:23-24). The commandment to "love your neighbor as yourself" was linked with and spoken of as being like the commandment to "love the Lord your God" (Matt. 22:37-40). Love of God and love of one's brother are two sides of the same coin, two aspects of the same relationship (1 John 2:10-11; 4:8, 20). Those who are committed to God in Christ are by the very fact of that commitment committed to love those whom God loves. They are committed to participation in the blessed community, the church.

# B. DECLINE OF GROUP LIFE IN MODERN SOCIETY

In contrast to the church with its inherent emphasis upon group life and togetherness, the world is experiencing a decline of interpersonal relations of depth and meaning. This is sometimes obscured for us by the fact that physically we have become more dependent upon one another. For example, in contrast to our pioneer forefathers, we are helpless

[2] Emil Brunner, op. cit., p. 11. Used by permission.

without the services of the grocer, the electrician, the milkman, and countless others. But this does not mean that we have any depth of relationship with these people. Quite the contrary; we are not as likely as before even to know the persons involved. We are being fragmented and isolated in our social and spiritual life, and the unity of our society is being destroyed. Amid this decline of personal relationship with others, effective small group action tends to disappear from the scene.

Kinship and tradition once were the characteristic bonds that held social groups together. People who had lived for generations in the same community and were related by blood knew each other intimately and participated frequently in relationships of depth of meaning. They shared common values and goals, and their relations with one another were natural and essential. But present-day society is increasingly characterized by voluntary social bonds and agreements by contract. We no longer associate chiefly with people whose entire background we know because they are our kin. We deal with many people whom we know only on the basis of the job they perform. The porter carries my baggage not because he loves me and is concerned about me, but because I pay him. I do not know who he is or how he lives, and I am queer by modern standards if I care to know.

The moving van has had its influence also. People change their place of residence more often. Many of the persons we meet at work and play, even when we are near home, do not share the same local traditions and value systems that we do. Added to this is a high degree of specialization and division of labor in society. In the simpler communities of a bygone day most men shared a common occupation. Even professional men often were also either farmers or craftsmen or both. But no longer is almost everyone engaged in similar or closely related occupations. This means that the life pattern* of others is not already known through familiarity with our own life pattern. Acquaintance, participation, and sharing must thus begin with the added handicap of great unfamiliarity.

Mass media of communication further complicate the pic-

* **LIFE PATTERN**—the way a person lives, his characteristic activities and experiences.

ture. No longer are political opinions and community decisions arrived at in free discussion among friends and neighbors in "Cy" Finch's general store, or in a democratic town meeting where each man's idea is important. People now arrive at opinions strongly influenced by the information and values disseminated through hundreds of thousands of identical copies of the daily newspaper or the weekly or monthly magazine, and through words and pictures reproduced millions of times over radio and TV. The free, face-to-face exchange of experience and opinion in the meaningful small group, which once was a key factor in the imparting of values and the shaping of opinions, tends to disappear. In a nation of nearly 200 million people one person's views seem to count for little.

Our efforts to combat this situation only lead to more depersonalization. We put ourselves and others into impersonal categories, and we seek to make our influence felt through large pressure groups. In our voluntary, mobile, mass society we tend toward what E. Durheim has called a "dust heap of individuals without links to one another."[3]

It is from such a world that Christians are called by God to be his people. Into it they are dispersed again to be his witnesses. It is a world in which persons tend to be reduced to contacts, prospects, operatives, subjects. A pretense of personalizing life is maintained. In the service club the man of the house is glad-handed, and the club rules require that he be called by his first name. But this is only a surface familiarity. His wife may read the gossip column and the human interest story and exchange small talk with the woman down the block; but this, too, fails to be the vibrant concern for persons as persons, which is so necessary for healthy personality development and so instrumental in the salvation of lost selves. Such a world needs a revival of personal groups. It needs the redemptive vital group life of the fellowship of the Holy Spirit.

## C. CHRISTIAN VALUES AND GROUP LIFE

Though the renewal of personal groups is so greatly needed in American life, we must not think that the group emphasis

[3] George C. Homans, *The Human Group*, Harcourt, Brace and Co., 1950, p. 457. Used by permission.

within the church is developed simply as an answer to the problem of modern society. The message of the gospel is not a weather vane response to currents of human thought. Rather the message of redemption is rich in values that apply to all human needs. In its various facets it fits modern man's need just as it did the different situation of earlier times. The gospel is thus adaptable and always applicable because it is not forever engraved on tablets of stone but transmitted through a living, vibrant community, the church.

Group participation is of the very nature of the church and the Christian commitment. The stress upon persons and groups which we need in our time is inherent in the values of our faith.

## 1. Personhood*

The importance of the person is a basic Christian value. Concern for persons in their own right and for their own sake has been a distinguishing characteristic of those who have been influenced by Christianity. God made us persons. Violating the personal integrity of others by self-assertion or by classifying and categorizing them is recognized as sinful. The Old Testament and the New are filled with incidents that set forth the importance of the individual.

"If we are persons, everyone is important in his own right. Cain is his brother's keeper. David cannot play fast and loose with Uriah and get away with it."[4]

The woman taken in adultery is not just an adulteress but a human being in need of redeeming love. Even the children who come seeking Jesus are persons and are, therefore, not to be brushed aside by the disciples but encouraged and invited to come to the Master.

The high value Christianity places on personhood means that no one can simply be put in a category or treated as a prospect or contact. No one can be run over roughshod or manipulated. Each one must be thought of as of real value and as having a contribution to make to the life of the group. It may not always be possible to see what an individual's

* PERSONHOOD—the state of being a person. Used here in connection with the importance of the individual personality. The concern for persons in their own right and for their own sake.

[4] Lowell B. Hazzard, "Where Two or Three," *International Journal of Religious Education*, Vol. 33, No. 9, p. 3. Used by permission.

contribution may be. His efforts to share in the discussion of a group problem or to aid in achieving a group goal may appear futile; yet those efforts are important to him as a person and, therefore, deserve consideration.

With this value of personhood in mind, group discussion ceases to be merely an opportunity to swap ideas and becomes a meeting of persons. In a board of trustees the pastor does not simply deal with board members and ideas about church property and finances. He deals with John Jones and Earl Williams and Herb Johnson. People cease to be mere audiences or classes as we begin to value them as individuals. A Sunday church school teacher does not teach a class, he teaches several different children who meet together in a class. In the church we develop a feeling of togetherness within which the desires, interests, and goals of each person interact with those of each other person, and the mutual personal encounter* becomes our group experiences.

## 2. Belongingness**

Everyone wants to belong, and in the Christian fellowship everyone does belong. No one is on the sidelines in the kingdom of God. Everyone participates. Each one is a part of God's people, a member of the body of Christ. He belongs because he is related to God in Christ. No longer is he a fugitive wanderer in the earth like Cain. Even though, like Abraham, he may be a sojourner in tents, he has the faith that he belongs to "the city which has foundations, whose builder and maker is God."

Zaccheus and Matthew were isolates. They were set apart from the group because they were hated tax collectors. One of the things Jesus did for them was to break their isolation. He identified himself with them. He ate with them. He included them among his followers. A part of their redemption involved their gaining a sense of belonging.

Of course the local church does not always succeed in giving everyone a sense of belonging. The church may be "run" by a small clique of influential individuals. The leadership

* ENCOUNTER—a meeting of minds in which there is recognition of mutual purposes and interests; the entering into deep personal relationship with another.
** BELONGINGNESS (sense of beloı.ging)—the feeling of being part of a group, a feeling that goes beyond having one's name on the membership list to thinking about the group in terms of "we."

38

clique may prevent others from gaining the experience necessary for leadership. In such a case, the failure of members to feel that they really belong is evident when they refer to church action with the word "they" instead of "we."

Just as Jesus despised no person but gave to those who followed him a feeling of belonging to the group, so his church must relate each person to his fellow believers and to the kingdom of God. The slavery of modern man to material things, to clothes, cars, TV, and all the other gadgets of our times is partly a response to the frustration of not belonging. The destruction of the unity of life has led men to establish superficial contact with more and more clubs and groups, but to be deeply involved in ever fewer of them or none at all. The recognition of his slavery to things has led man to assert his individuality in his effort to escape. He vainly tries to be different and separate from others. But freedom from slavery to things comes not in more individualization but in more social responsibility and relatedness, and relatedness comes in commitment to Christ.

> "Remember that you were at that time separated from Christ, . . . having no hope and without God in the world. But now in Christ Jesus you who once were far off have been brought near in the blood of Christ. . . . So then you are no longer strangers and sojourners, but you are fellow citizens with the saints and members of the household of God" (Eph. 2:12-13, 19).

## 3. Community

The very fact that God has laid the foundation of our common life and bound us together in one body makes community a basic Christian value. Love must be revealed in relationship. The witness must be a community witness. God has given us brethren who live by his call and promise, and the life together becomes our joy and our strength.

> "Christian brotherhood is not an ideal which we must realize; it is rather a reality created by God in Christ in which we may participate."[5]

Community, that small unit of society in which the members have a firsthand knowledge of each other and share a

[5] Dietrich Bonhoeffer, *Life Together*, Harper and Brothers, 1954, p. 30. Used by permission.

common life together, has been disappearing in our times. Small units have been replaced by larger ones. We do not have firsthand knowledge of each other when we know each other only as functionaries. A child places two blocks together and those two blocks are in contact at many points. But when he places two balls together they touch each other at only one point. Our firsthand knowledge of each other is limited because we touch each other only at an occasional point rather than sharing a common life.

Under these circumstances problems of conflicting values and interests increase. The informal consensus* of community is gone. In our effort to fill the resulting void we resort more and more to laws and force to achieve and maintain standards of conduct, and we find them less and less effective.

In Christianity we find a new community. The experience which Christians have with God and with one another unites them in a new common life. The life they share together takes unquestioned primacy for them. It is a community which is not of this world. But Christians who belong to this new community are under orders not to withdraw from the world. They are to continue their daily walk in contact with those outside the fellowship showing love and concern for them. Their new vocation is to witness to the purpose of God for human redemption in everything they do and say. They show and tell that the rule of God in human hearts is a realizable fact and that only in that fact lies the true happiness and the perfect community which all men seek.

## D. CIRCLES OF INVOLVEMENT

Ideally every Christian is equally involved in the church. One has experienced the redeeming love and mercy of God as much as another. Faith and commitment have come through personal contact with the Christian group. Personhood, belongingness, and community have become ruling values in the life of each. The people of God are one, and each belongs to the witnessing fellowship.

A very brief contact with actual Christians in a local church, however, is enough to bring us to a more realistic

* CONSENSUS—when agreement is reached among all members of a group. Even when general agreement is reached and the minority agrees that the decision of the majority be adopted, it might be considered that consensus has been reached.

view. Not all Christians are, in fact, equally involved in the church. Some may have "joined" without any real commitment. The commitment of some may not have been the full and total one which the action of God should call forth in us. The commitment of others may not have been strengthened by the continuing relationships in personal groups needed for the nurture of the "new creature in Christ Jesus." The previous experience of the Christian may have left scars that hamper his full participation; or the local church itself may be so formalized and institutionalized that the same bases of participation prevail in the church as in the secular world. Whatever the reason, the relation of persons to the church range from mere marginal contact to deep personal concern.

This is the same situation Jesus faced in his earthly ministry. When he spoke to the "men of Galilee," some who heard him were indifferent or opposed. No one would suppose that the curious thousands who came out to hear him by the sea or witnessed his miracles were as much concerned as the seventy he sent out two by two. Even closer to the center were the twelve who were the chief working group of the Master. And those three intimate friends, Peter, James, and John, who went to the Mount of Transfiguration, were the fellowship of the deeply concerned.

The relationship of people to the church can be described in terms of concentric circles. Within the mass of the generally opposed or unconcerned are the constituents of the church, those who for one reason or another have shown some interest: they may have permitted their children to attend the Sunday church school; they may have called on the services of the minister in time of death; they may have attended services, or have members of their family in the church membership.

Somewhat closer to the core of things are the members of the church. At some time they have taken a definite step of identification with the church, though some of them may show as few signs of interest as those in the broader constituency. Some churches find it useful to describe an active membership circle within the total membership, though considerable exception might be taken to the criteria used to define "active." At least, all would recognize that some mem-

# CIRCLES OF INVOLVEMENT

## a. In Jesus' day

"YE MEN OF GALLILEE"

THE SEVENTY

THOSE ON THE MOUNT

THE TWELVE

THE FIVE THOUSAND

THE CONSTITUENCY

ACTIVE PARTICIPANTS

FELLOWSHIP OF THE CONCERNED

MEMBERS

THE SECULAR COMMUNITY

bers are more involved than others both in the activity of the church as an institution and in the attempt to exemplify and proclaim their faith.

But the circle of those who have really "been with Jesus," who are deeply concerned and can and do give real expression to their faith, is the smallest circle of all. They are the ones who explore the deeper meanings of their commitment. They are the core of vital Christianity within the church. They experience the "real togetherness which makes effective witness possible."[6]

This is what Tom Allan and others have described as a "Church within the Church."[7]

## E. THE FELLOWSHIP OF THE CONCERNED*

This core of vital Christianity cannot be established in a church by passing a resolution or adding an organization. It must be there as an expression of the concern of those who take their faith and commitment seriously. The people who are deeply affected can be discovered and developed into a fellowship of the concerned which can grow to become the nucleus of the Christian community.

Tom Allan, a British minister, found that members of his parish who were asked to go out on a visitation campaign were not articulate about their faith. They wanted to witness to people, but they could not express themselves. They found it necessary to undertake a serious study of their faith. But more than that, they developed a fellowship of prayer and discussion which came to be increasingly essential to them. This became a "Church within the Church," a real fellowship of the concerned.

The need for such a community of faith and sharing is felt by many and for various reasons. Donald, a young pastor, recently expressed his concern that he had not been working with anything really basic in the lives of his people. His pastorate has been successful if measured by membership, finances, organization, and program; but he is dissatisfied. Program and activities just scratch the surface. Adding members,

[6] D. Elton Trueblood, op. cit., p. 8.
[7] Tom Allan, The Face of My Parish, Harper and Brothers, 1957, p. 51.
* FELLOWSHIP OF THE CONCERNED—a group of people deeply affected by their experience of God and seeking to witness together to the life and reality of the living Christ.

he knows, may not be the same as building the kingdom of God. He is tired of being a "bush beater." He wants his ministry to have a spiritual and not just an organizational impact. He wants to stop nursing along an organization and start building the body of Christ.

Jane is a member of a large church and is a regular and active participant. She comes away from an impersonal, anonymous, urban society to a church in which she hopes to find the blessed community, the people of God. Instead, she worships with people who don't know each other. She finds that they continue to keep from knowing each other by hiding week after week behind masks of piousness. She yearns for a fellowship of real sharing.

Frank is a young man who is seeking to explore the implications of his faith for his life work. He does not want to be preached at. He wants an opportunity to think through his vocation with others facing the same decision. He wants a group that will not just criticize and condemn, but one that will share with him in such a way that he will be encouraged and strengthened to apply his faith to this major decision in life.

Tony is indignant about the injustice and inhumanity in the world around him. But people in the church, he finds, are preoccupied with a conception of sin that covers primarily personal vices. He needs a group of like faith and commitment to help him explore the relevance of Christianity to the problems of economic, political, and international life. He also needs a group that will help him discover the fears and hostilities within his own personality that account for part of his indignation. He needs to share in a real communion of the saints.

Each of these four, and there are many more, is seeking a fellowship of the concerned. In his or her own local church there may be others with similar needs; but there is no communication on the level of concerns. The church as a whole is failing to be such a fellowship, and the groups within the church are failing to accomplish the depth of sharing needed to actualize a fellowship of the concerned. For this reason a number of churches have moved to form new groups variously called "cell groups," "prayer groups," or "neighborhood yoke fellowships." These groups avoid the usual organizational pattern and direct their attention to devotional practices and deep interpersonal relationships. They become the church within the church.

We are not suggesting a sanctimonious inner circle. No "holier-than-thou" attitude is appropriate among Christians. Pride in spiritual attainments is selfishness. It is a relic of the old life of bondage to sin and self from which Christ has freed us. A fellowship of the concerned is more an expression of need than of virtue or spirituality. It expresses the need for devotional exercise, spiritual discipline, mutual encouragement, and the sharing of insights and social concerns.

The need for a fellowship with depth of interpersonal relations does not necessarily call for the creating of new groups within the church. It is both possible and quite sensible for the small church as a whole, or for existing groups within the larger church, to meet this need. In most cases, however, they will have to become much more direct and personal in character and much more deeply spiritual in orientation than at present.

## F. RELATIONSHIPS IN THE CHRISTIAN GROUP

As church members we live in the same highly segmented society as the rest of the world. We tend to know each other only in functional relationships. We know people for what they do, not for what they are. When someone speaks in a church group or is nominated for an office, all too often we have to ask, "Who is he?" "What does he do?" or comment, "I didn't know he was a member of our church." Groups which are effective in redemptive witness and in changing persons must be small enough and personal enough to enable us to "get all the way around" and to fill out our relationships with each other person by direct interaction with him. Only when we can do this, can we have a full appreciation of the attitudes, values, and degrees of satisfaction of each member of the group. Such full appreciation is needed for group solidarity; but, even more, such appreciation makes the contribution that each unique individual brings to the group more fully effective in the development of each other person.

In the small rural church in the stable community of a bygone day this was not so difficult. There the life pattern of others was already known through familiarity with one's own life pattern; the backgrounds of others were known through knowledge of their families and community tradition; and the experiences of others were known through the sharing of a common life with them. But now, out of our impersonal society, we come together in the church, whether it is rural or urban, with little knowledge of the life patterns, backgrounds, and experiences of others. The difficulty of establishing and filling out our interpersonal relationships is tremendously increased. We need more time for sharing and, instead, have less. The frequency of church meetings has been declining. So has the length of services. In some churches the two hours of "church and Sunday church school" on Sunday morning are the extent of the week's meetings. If a midweek service is held, most members do not participate in it.

Furthermore, the services are increasingly more formal and do not permit a maximum of fellowship, thus not contributing much to personal acquaintance. Even the adult Sunday church school class is too big, too teacher-dominated, and too filled with platitudes to accomplish much of an interpersonal nature. The testimony meeting is either gone entirely or has become too stereotyped to be personally meaningful.

Christians like Donald, Jane, Frank, and Tony may seek in vain in the church for the dynamic togetherness of a fellowship of the concerned; for in the face of a segmented, impersonal society, the church has all too often failed to maintain the highly personal character of its life as a community. Yet the need is there in the lives of church members, and as other aspects of their lives lose their face-to-face quality that need becomes greater. Those who are conscious of their need seek more opportunities for depth of interpersonal communication in the church.

The desire for opportunity to share Christian experience does not represent a prying curiosity about other people's inner lives. It represents, rather, a recognition of the need for mutuality. Our faith moves through personal groups in which the power of the Spirit functions. Christianity is more an experience than a dogma, more a commitment than a creed. It is transmitted from one person to another, and personal relations in small groups are the key to its transmission.

But important as good personal relations in the church are, they are not what makes church groups differ from all other groups. The really distinguishing work is that the social relationships established in a church group are not just with human persons. The church is composed of persons related to God in Christ. It operates in the recognition of the presence of God. He is present not just in his creation but also in the fellowship. The power and effectiveness of what happens in the Christian group cannot be explained in terms of human effort. Through his Holy Spirit, God is in the group as the Great Person. He gives new life to those he has redeemed from self and death, and they respond with joyful praise and love and service. Worship thus becomes a key activity of the Christian fellowship. It comes naturally as an expression of continual wonder and joy that the great God of the universe, the Creator of the ends of the earth, should reveal himself to sinful, recalcitrant men and give of himself, suffering the death of the cross, for their redemption. The worship of the church is an ever renewed expression of humility, joyful praise, and dedication.

Naturally the Christian group opens its meeting with prayer. It does this not just because it is customary, not because there is a minister present to do it, but because of the awareness that God is there, in the midst of them. The members talk with God. They talk with one another about God, too, for the group helps each member to a fuller understanding of him. The divine Personality is so rich and full that no one person's experience is sufficient to encompass it. We must share our experiences of God with one another in order that we may know more of him whom to know is life everlasting. It is this divine fellowship which makes the feeling of belonging to the church so satisfying that no other group membership could possibly take its place. The fact that there are those who do not find it so satisfying is a condemnation not of them, but of the church. The church has failed to make God real to them. It has failed to share with them the vital experience of his presence and work in the life of the church.

## G. EXPANDING THE CIRCLES

Before we conclude our discussion of the group life of the church, a caution needs to be added. We have emphasized circles of involvement within the Christian group. However, we should not be misled into thinking that the purpose of the church is centered in itself. The church does not exist to hold meetings or to create a little closely knit fellowship.

God loves the whole world. Christ died for the world, not just for the few persons in it who already acknowledge him. The very nature of the church is mission. It is called into being to witness.

"All this is from God, who through Christ reconciled us to himself and gave us the ministry of reconciliation; that is, God was in Christ reconciling the world to himself, not counting their trespasses against them, and entrusting to us the message of reconciliation" (2 Cor. 5:18-19).

The lines we have drawn to represent the circles of involvement must not be thought of as barriers. The circles of influence of the gospel must be made ever wider. Those who are outside the circles must learn of the redeeming love of God. Those whose relationships are peripheral must be drawn into the innermost circle. The unconcerned must become the fellowship of the concerned, the intimate friends of the Master.

The truly witnessing church points men to Christ. It does not reach out to others simply to draw them to itself. Yet, the quality of its fellowship greatly affects its witness.

Our ministry of reconciliation is best accomplished through face-to-face groups. These must be groups that welcome new persons and give recognition and a sense of belongingness to each one. They must be groups whose atmosphere encourages sharing at a depth level our experience of God in Christ. They must also be groups in which there reigns a spirit of unity.

The Master prayed "that they may all be one; . . . so that the world may believe that thou hast sent me" (John 17:21). The oneness of the group is essential to our witness. To some this suggests an organizational or creedal unity. Fragmented organization or cleavages resulting from differing formulations of our faith certainly are destructive to the unity of the church. But singleness of organization or creed does not insure the solidarity which the church needs. Nor does oneness come simply from the democratic principle of majority rule. The togetherness and accord of the church are based upon divine reconciliation. Where the group is gathered by the Lord and his Spirit is experienced in the members' sharing of their faith, their Christian experience, and their concerns, there will be unity of spirit and the oneness the Master prayed for.

We have said that size may be a factor in the group character of a church. However, the fact that a local church is large does not necessarily mean that there cannot be unity. Small groups in such a church can develop a basic togetherness within themselves which is related to the larger fellowship. Each group can help to do this by recognizing itself as a part of the Christian community.

The church, too, can foster a spirit of unity by effectively co-ordinating its group program and making its large public services a vital expression of the faith and fellowship experienced in the small groups. A church council which takes an over-all view of the church program, frequent opportunities for sharing among the leaders of the church's groups, and a parish zone system which facilitates expression of Christian concern for all the people of an area whether they are in the church or not — all these contribute to the total unity of the church and broaden the togetherness achieved in its small face-to-face groups.

## Questions for Discussion

1. What barriers are there to real togetherness in your church?

2. How do the concepts of personhood, belongingness, and community affect the relation of the Christian with other people?

3. By what actions should a church demonstrate to its members that they belong to God?

4. How can the church "make God real" to people?

5. What is the value of sharing experiences with thers through conversation?

6. Where is the "fellowship of the concerned" in your church?

## Suggested Reading

*The Face of My Parish*, Tom Allan, Harper and Brothers, New York, 1957.

A British pastor writes of the discovery of a "church within a church" and the resulting changes in his parish ministry.

*Life Together*, Dietrich Bonhoeffer, Harper and Brothers, New York, 1954.

This heroic Christian, martyred by the Nazis during World War II, writes of the deep meaning of the Christian community. The reader cannot but be stirred by this book.

*Living As Comrades*, Daniel Johnson Fleming, Agricultural Missions, New York, 1950.

Chapter I is an effective discussion of Christian community. The balance of the book illustrates the effects of community and Christian sharing from the experiences of missionaries.

*The Human Group*, George C. Homans, Harcourt, Brace and Co., New York, 1950.

Chapter 18, "Groups and Civilization."

*In But Not of the World*, Robert W. Spike, Association Press, New York, 1957.

This book dramatically contrasts the biblical image of the church with actual practice in the life of the Christian and in the local church.

*The Meaning of Persons*, Paul Tournier, Harper and Brothers, New York, 1957.

*Herein Is Love*, Reuel L. Howe, Judson Press, Valley Forge, Pa., 1961

## IV

# Groups at Work in the Church

The church is a group when it is small enough and personal enough for a considerable amount of mutuality and togetherness to develop within it. This does not rule out groups in churches of large membership. In such cases, and even in some smaller churches, it might be more correct to say that the church contains groups. These groups maintain many of the elements of real fellowship that exist in the church. In the sense that the church is a fellowship they are *the church*, the fellowship of the redeemed.

Since there may be many of these groups within a local congregation, each of them which has within it a true fellowship of the redeemed may want to look upon itself as a church. Such a view would lead to unwarranted fragmentation. A Sunday church school class, a youth fellowship, a women's circle, and a cell group are not each little churches. They are, however, specific manifestations of the church. The local church is a community composed of young and old, of individuals, and of whole families. It is the

"local gathered community of those who have responded to God's call and have covenanted themselves together as a congregation of God's people."[1]

The groups within the church are interest groups, often composed of a small number of persons of the same age and interest. To the extent that these smaller groups look upon themselves as witnessing groups and share the redemptive task of the church, they are organs of the body of Christ. They may not be churches, but they are the church at work.

We must now look more closely at these groups and at the work of the church in light of the understandings of group behavior which have come to us from the social sciences.

[1] Robert T. Handy, *op. cit.*, p. 61.

## A. THE FUNCTIONS OF GROUPS

Groups may be organized for many purposes. The purpose of a group is what is intended by those who organize and/or participate in it. Sometimes these purposes are clear and explicit; sometimes they are confused or hidden, and they may even be forgotten. We shall not attempt a list of purposes, for such a list could at best be only partial. New purposes are being thought up every day and new groups formed around them.

Much more fruitful for our exploration is the function of groups. The function of a group is what the group actually does in relation to its own life, its individual members, and the other groups around it. Purpose involves intention. Function is what actually happens or is accomplished, regardless of whether intended or not. The functions of groups can be rather conveniently classified under three main headings: groups (1) meet the needs of individuals, (2) work toward group goals, and (3) work for group maintenance.

### 1. Meeting the Needs of Individuals

We have pointed out in Chapter I something of the interrelation between the person and the group. Each person brings to the group a great wealth of experience that has shaped him as an individual personality. At the same time the group in which he participates is bringing to him many new influences which affect and shape his personality so that we may say in truth that the person is a product of his group.

Each person comes into a group with personal needs to be met. Some of these needs are the result of unsatisfactory experience in other groups, and some of them are simply the result of the fact that we are social beings and as such have normal needs that can only be met in group experience. One of these is the need for acceptance,* for belongingness. The child who says, "The other kids don't like me"; the youth who admits, "I wasn't invited"; and the adult who says, "I don't think the boss knows I am around," are all giving expression to the frustration experienced when this need is not met.

* ACCEPTANCE—a sense of being wholeheartedly accepted by all the members of a group; to feel that I am wanted, accepted, and that I belong.

Another need is the need for security. A child whose parents had moved to another state, first to a temporary residence and then to a permanent one, had been on a day's outing with the family. As they were returning home at evening, the child looked at his father and asked, "Where are we going?" "Home," was the simple reply. But it wasn't that simple to the child. His next question, "Which home?" showed his basic feeling of insecurity resulting from the family move. Fortunately this child was not greatly disturbed, for he had a strong sense of security within the family group. Others may not be so fortunate.

People come to groups for the satisfaction of their need for security, but they also come with fear and distrust. They don't know whether the group will accept them; they are uncertain about their own behavior; and they may even fear that the group will swallow them up. All these fears stand in the way of the very security the group participant seeks. Church groups are not without their causes for fear. The Sunday church school class of small children may frighten an inexperienced teacher. The necessity to stand and speak before a group may frighten an adult church member. Both young and old need a feeling of security, and this need may be met or frustrated by the group.

Variety or new experience is another personal need which the group may satisfy. Certainly one of the reasons for the popularity of fraternal organizations among people whose occupations are routine and monotonous is the variety which these groups bring into their lives. The man who has become a slave of a machine and whose clothes, because of the nature of his work, have to be like those of everyone else on the job, can have a grand title at the lodge, wear a fancy plumed hat, and be greeted with honor and dignity for a change. It may not be the intended purpose of the church group to bring variety into the lives of its members, but for some members it may serve this function, among others.

We could go on illustrating personal needs with a list longer than space here permits. The need for recognition, the need for self-expression, the need to participate, the need for mental stimulation, the need to be freed from guilt feelings, and many others may figure in group participation. The needs of the persons who come into church groups are not unlike the needs of those who join any group in society. The need which is fulfilled for a boy by the delinquent gang is the same need fulfilled by the scout troop or the church youth fellowship. If our groups are to operate effectively, they will have to take the needs of individual members into account and in some way integrate the meeting of those needs with the goals of the group. If our groups do this, we may speak of them as person-centered groups.

## 2. Working Toward Goals

Frequently a group has goals outside the group itself. Problem solving is one such goal. In the case of a committee, the problem may be stated at the time the group is set up — "Mr. President, I move that a committee be appointed to find the source of the pollution that is killing the fish in Roaring River." In other groups the problem may appear long after the group's beginning — "During the remainder of the class session today I think we ought to talk about what we can do to stop the selling of pernicious literature to school children in our town."

In addition to problem solving, a group may work toward goal attainment. The athletic team seeks to win the pennant, the political party seeks to win the election. The goal of the Sunday church school class may be that of imparting knowledge of the Bible, while that of the missionary society may be collecting materials and funds for the missionary enterprise. Some groups have many projects. Others have to cast around for projects to undertake. A group which has no goals and has to go out hunting for projects is probably in serious difficulty and may be dying.

Sometimes goal attainment may stand in the way of meeting individual needs. This may be clearly seen in the choir director who would attain the goal of high quality music by using only the most talented members of the choir, but who has to deal with less talented individuals whose need for participation must also be met. What athletic coach has not asked, Should we use only the best players on the team and thus win, or should we give everyone a chance to play? Sometimes this conflict is more apparent than real, for giving all the players a chance may develop players who will win future games for the team. Should we ask the minister to lead the devotions, as one lay woman put it, "Because he is the best qualified person to do it," or should we ask different lay people and give them the challenge and experience of developing a devotional thought for themselves and the group?

The goal of the church is the proclamation of the gospel. This is its mission. This is the task for which God's people are commissioned. Church groups may have more specific tasks to perform, but their ultimate goal of witnessing must never be forgotten.

### 3. Group Maintenance

Many of the activities and concerns of the group are devoted to its own inner workings, structure, membership, and other factors related to the group's maintaining itself. These are important. The group cannot meet the needs of members it does not have, nor can it attain goals or solve problems if it ceases to exist as a group. Maintenance includes such questions as: Do we have a regular order of procedure? What can we do to increase attendance? Why aren't we recruiting new members? Who would make a good secretary? But groups can concentrate so much on this sort of function that they have little time and energy for anything else. This seems to have been the case with the organized women's Sunday church school class which has as its motto, "Keep on keeping on!"

Groups show their immaturity when they spend a major portion of their time in "housekeeping problems," that is, taking roll, reading the minutes, hearing reports, and other routine business. Members of a college faculty studying the records of faculty meetings were amazed to discover that they had spent more than half of the time in their faculty meetings conducting routine business, when they might have been seriously facing the challenge of the educational tasks before them. In contrast to such immature groups, mature groups find group maintenance no serious problem. They handle "group housekeeping" with a minimum of time and effort and even cope with serious problems without major disruption of the group.

Some groups' only goals are maintenance goals. The end

they strive for is to maintain some group or institution. A sociologist making a study of community organizations recently classified local PTA groups under the heading, "Help school and teacher." Ladies Aids came under the heading, "Help church and preacher." If the only goal of a group is that of helping to maintain some other group, it will be faced with two difficulties. First, it may sometimes find itself out of agreement with the group it is sponsoring and thus face frustration. Second, it will find its program rather sterile, for all its goals have to be achieved indirectly through the other group.

Here again we need to note a possible conflict between functions. Working toward group goals may not contribute to group maintenance. Taking on certain tasks may alienate some members of the group. More than one church has had to face this when it has taken a firm stand on racial integration, slum clearance, or some other social issue. Members have left churches over such matters as the missionary enterprise, co-operation with other denominations, the choice of Sunday church school literature, or the introduction of social innovations into the church program. Such problems are especially difficult where the group is dependent for its support upon those who take exception to the group goals. Fear of upsetting those who do not share completely the values of the group may sometimes prevent the group from taking any action.

These problems need to be frankly faced by a group if it is going to maintain itself in good working condition. We have to recognize that sometimes the rigid stand of a stubborn member may be more an expression of personal need than of principle. The opposition raised to the building program by Bill Balk may melt away when he is given proper recognition for the efforts he has already exerted, or when some other personal need of his is met.

## B. PERSON-CENTERED AND TASK-CENTERED GROUPS IN THE CHURCH

Church groups ought to be mature enough to concern themselves with more than group maintenance and be able to emphasize the other two goals. They should either be person-centered — that is, focused on the needs of individual persons and on relations of persons with one another, or task-centered — that is, focused on projects, goals, or programs.

Sunday church school classes should be person-centered. The best teachers do not teach lessons, they teach persons. Their purpose is not so much to impart certain information as to help the students learn, think, develop, and know the impact of Christ upon their lives.

> "The Sunday church school teacher must do more than teach religious truth. He must be a cultivator of Christian fellowship. He must seek to reproduce in his class the kind of personal relationships and feelings of 'group-ness' which characterizes the true church of Jesus Christ."[2]

The adult class may be only remotely interested in studying the lesson. The members may be chiefly interested in the pleasure of each other's company. The Sunday church school session simply gives them a good excuse for meeting at regular intervals.

Many groups in the church are both task and person-centered. The Woman's Society may have a task of raising funds and preparing supplies for missionaries at work in distant places. But it also plays a major role in the development of persons in a broadening conception of their task as Christians.

Many groups in the church are by their very nature task-centered. The board of trustees has a task to perform in the care of the church property. Its realm of responsibility may be clearly set forth in the church constitution. A committee also may be assigned a specific task. The choir is another task-centered group. It has the important job of taking a leading role in the worship services of the church.

But not all choirs are entirely task-centered. Members of the choir may constitute one of the real fellowship groups of the church. With a concern for others, as well as a concern for good music, the choir members have an active part in evangelistic outreach and effectively contribute to the growth of Christian persons.

A committee also may be person-centered. An interesting example is that of the Community Festival committee of the village of Alexandria, Ohio. When this committee was as-

[2] Kenneth L. Cober, *Evangelism in the Sunday Church School*, The Judson Press, 1955, p. 29.

signed the task of preparing the centennial celebration for this small rural community, it agreed on the principle of distributing responsibility as broadly as possible to include as many people as possible. With the attention thus turned toward persons, the committee arranged every part of the preparation and celebration in such a way as to give many individuals a share. The result was that in a village of five hundred people more than one hundred and fifty shared committee responsibilities. They enjoyed working together so much that they didn't want to wait a quarter of a century before doing it again. Now every five years the community stages a summer festival featuring total community participation. There is no commercialism, and all leadership is local. In their 1955 "Festival of Youth" nine people served on the general committee which co-ordinated the work of twenty-one active task-centered committees involving many individuals. If one could total all those who had parts in the play, built floats for the parade, prepared food for the dinners, and so on, the record of active participation would be even larger. The point, of course, is not just the number participating, but the fact that broad participation was the result of the refusal on the part of the committee to be entirely task-centered.

One of the problems of the midweek service in many churches is that no one knows what its purpose is. Is it task-centered? Is it for the purpose of holding a service in the middle of the week? A prominent church in one of our midwestern cities found that when its program was guided by a greater concern for persons, the character of its midweek service changed. An actual list of the things done in the service does not sound very different from the usual pattern: hymn singing, sharing, Bible study, prayer. But there is a new expectancy and power. The singing is kept informal and the Bible study simple. Emphasis is placed on the sharing, and the attempt is made to make the period of prayer as personal and direct as possible. The result, says the pastor, is a new depth of relationship because people are being real to each other, exposing themselves to God and each other in a way they had but rarely done before.

# C. THE REDEMPTIVE TASK OF CHURCH GROUPS

Every church group is the church at work. Each group within the local church, to the extent that it is a fellowship of the redeemed, is the church. As such, it partakes of the task of the church.

"The ultimate purpose of all Church groups, regardless of what the immediate purpose may be, must be conceived of, in some measure, as an attempt to effect encounter with the living God, or to follow up from that encounter in study, fellowship, and action."[8]

In the church, all groups — study groups, action groups, committees, boards, and classes — act under a commission to proclaim the good news, as God provides ability and opportunity. "You are the salt of the earth." "Go into all the world." The church group is a redemptive group. In other words, no matter what the goal of a task-centered church group, it will not be true to its calling as a part of the church unless it is at least to some extent person-centered. Even the board of trustees and the finance committee must think of their work in terms of redemptive purpose. They must be implementing the concern of the entire congregation for the proclaiming of the gospel, and they must be carrying out their work in such ways that the people who come into contact with the church through them will be aware of the Spirit of God in their lives.

The very nature of the church is its mission to witness. The failure to perceive this truth concerning the church has led to two related misconceptions among Christians. One is to think of only those who go to foreign or disadvantaged places as missionaries. The second is to consider only those activities of the church evangelistic which include a verbal appeal. Some progress has been made in that we recognize that medical doctors, agriculturalists, educators, and others can be missionaries, as well as preachers and Bible teachers. But the average layman has not broadened the term "missionary" to include himself in his everyday activity. The meaning of the term "evangelism" has tended to become increasingly specialized for us. In many churches it is tied to a method of appealing for a decision, and the church is thought to be

[8] Howard Grimes, *op. cit.*, p. 111. Used by permission.

evangelistic if a revival meeting is held, an invitation is given at the close of the service, or a visitation campaign is conducted at regular intervals.

God's calling to man places every aspect of his daily life as parent, worker, citizen, churchman, consumer, spectator, neighbor under the divine imperative. As a committed Christian the individual must proclaim the lordship of Christ over every area of life. Therefore every activity in which he is engaged and every role that he plays ought to be an act of proclaiming this lordship and, for that reason, evangelistic.

When this is understood, the church, the fellowship of committed persons, becomes a fellowship of evangelists. Not only does the Lord's Supper "proclaim the Lord's death until he comes"; every service of the church in which the praises of God are sung for his wonderful works among the children of men, is a proclamation of the good news. Knowing the mercy, the grace, and the love of God "in that while we were yet sinners Christ died for us," how can we but proclaim that redemption? The corporate worship of the church, the *koinonia* (fellowship or communion) of the saints, our common life together, and our outgoing acts of Christian love — all these must portray the love of God in Christ for the world. Every act of the church and every act of a group within the church must witness to redemption. Going through the forms of worship and study does not proclaim redemption. Redemption is proclaimed by the vital relationships of redeemed persons. Church groups must be person-centered and must reveal the redeeming love of God in a winsome and compelling way in and to the life of persons. No church group can be a part of the church and ignore the fact that the church was called to witness. It must think of its relation to that redemptive task.

## D. GROUPS NEW AND OLD

We work through existing groups in the church. Each church, depending on its historic tradition and its unique experience, has a group structure already established. There may be many groups or few. These may be large or small, effective or ineffective. Each person in a church is heir to the group structure of that church. Aware of this, one cynic described his own large downtown church in this manner: "Central Church is a collection of organizations that meet on Sunday morning to sell tickets to each other." This was hardly fair to the deeply spiritual people who participated in some groups in that church, but it suggests the problem of the existing group structure.

Some of the existing groups in the church may have lost their vitality. A small rural church had two women's organizations, a Ladies Aid and a Missionary Society. The older women belonged to the Aid and the younger to the Missionary Society. Eventually the older women became too feeble and too few to carry on their regular program. They recruited no new members and found it necessary to hold their meetings in conjunction with the Missionary Society. The Ladies Aid was a group that had lost its vitality and was no longer able to function, but it still persisted and had to be reckoned with in any effort to deal with the program of that church.

Other groups may have become so entangled with a tradition of ineffectuality that they may have to be by-passed. One small church whose board of trustees didn't take care of its building, established a building committee to maintain the church property. It continued to elect a board of trustees, however, even though the board did nothing, since its major function had been transferred to another group.

Good groups are made, not born. The committees, boards, classes, and groups of a church cannot be allowed just to exist. They must be worked at and developed. Some will have to alter their character entirely. Others, with minor modifications in their organization and functioning, will continue to meet the needs of persons and fulfill their redemptive mission. Still others may have to go out of existence entirely. New groups will have to be established, not just to replace old groups, but to meet needs which have been unmet.

Aging is a factor calling for group modification. After reaching adulthood, people prefer not to be promoted from class to class as they were as children and young people in the Sunday church school. This means that classes grow old along with their members, and the life history of the adult department includes the gradual liquidating of older classes and the adding of new classes for new young adults.

Customarily we have used age as a means of dividing persons into small groups of similar interests and experiences. But with the accelerated pace of cultural change, the same space of years chronologically may mean a greater difference in experience today than it did in the past. Sociologists have suggested that this may be one of the reasons why it is more difficult for parents now to understand the world of their children than it was a generation or two ago. The distance between young adults and adults is wider also. This world of rapid change calls for more effective sharing between persons of different ages and thus for more personal groups in the church.

At the same time, much of life today reduces our relationships to impersonal contacts. John Casteel has pointed out that even God is thought of as impersonal "Power," people as "prospects," and that we understand ourselves only as we are "processed."[4] This increasingly impersonal character of society puts demand on the church for more personal groups with their face-to-face meetings and their real exchange of experiences, needs, and insights. If a church doesn't have groups which provide for such mutuality, it needs to get them either by modifying its present group pattern or by the adding of new groups. The changing needs of people, the changing functions of institutions, and the changing social situation call for a restudy of the group life of the church.

## E. GROUP OUTREACH

A group which is having a vital experience of deep fellowship and sharing will be attractive to others. Some will hear about such a group and seek it out. Others may crave for the experience the group could provide, but for one reason or another, ranging all the way from traditions to the fear of how the group may respond to them, will not seek the group unless they are themselves sought. Every church group is related to the mission of the church, which is a seeking, witnessing mission. God has chosen to reveal himself, and those who are his people are called to reach out to others with the message of the self-revealing God. Church groups of voluntary membership (boards and committees excepted, of course)

4 John L. Casteel, *op. cit.*, p. 19.

must continue to reach new people if they are to be true to their calling. Their vocation is evangelism.

The vocation of the Christian is the exercise of his call from God to witness to the grace and mercy of God as revealed in Jesus Christ. In every way in which he is involved in the world—his job, his community, his recreation, his family life — he has the opportunity to live out his faithfulness to Christ. His life in the group is a part of this witness, as together with other Christians he seeks to discover what God is doing now in their lives and in the life of the world. The group is a living fellowship of faith within the world. Christians ought never to think of themselves as being a group separated from the world, but must always seek to demonstrate the openness of their community of faith, so that others may be moved to join in its life.

Just how each group will proceed to reach new people will depend upon the nature of the group and what methods are considered appropriate for it. But each one, regardless of its methods, needs to have a working plan for winning others.

Church groups will do well to study the principles for outreach developed in the National Christian Teaching Mission program of fellowship evangelism.[5] One of these principles is that each group needs to develop and maintain a responsibility list. This will be an up-to-date list of persons for whom the group assumes spiritual responsibility. Names on this list will come from a variety of sources: from members of the group itself, suggestions made to the group by other people, available lists of persons of the particular age or interest which this group represents, the total constituency list of the church, a religious census, and other sources.

The church in the large complex community containing many churches and church groups will assemble its list from various sources. The church in the small rural community, however, needs to think in terms of its responsibility for the spiritual life of the people of the entire area in which it may be the only functioning church or, at best, one of a very few.

A second principle involves the cultivation of that responsibility list. This may be done by an individual approach in which a member of the group calls on someone whose name

[5] Harry C. Munro, *op. cit.*

appears on the list. Use may also be made of existing occasions for fellowship, study, and service to attract new persons to the group. But groups which invite new people to meetings will do well to give considerable attention to the nature of those meetings. Probably each of us knows at least one group whose meetings are so deadly that one visit is enough to frighten even the most interested person away.

Cultivation may also be carried on through a specialized approach. This has been the goal of the mass evangelism meeting. Many churches have discovered, however, that the people they have responsibility for will not come to a church service aimed directly at them. Some have met this problem through what have been called "evangelistic house parties" in which persons who are the group's responsibility are invited to the home of a member of the group for an evening. There, in an informal atmosphere, a free and honest discussion of the meaning of their faith and their common experience of it by members of the group invites new persons to explore the possibility of their own commitment and participation in the church.

Because a church may have many groups, each with a sense of sharing in the total mission of the church, some sort of co-ordination of responsibilities is needed.

"Ways must be found in which many groups can share in planning and decision-making. Two-way communication between groups, and between church leaders and groups, must be provided. Only in this way can the total church, through the medium of many and varied groups, carry out its function as a redeeming, serving, worshipping, fellowship." [6]

Size is not always an adequate measure of whether a group is satisfactorily fulfilling its task. One group may be small and be kept small for a purpose. Another group may be large and still not be reaching all it should. Its very size may, in fact, be the root of its failure to reach others. Study of the growth cycle of groups indicates that groups tend to reach a saturation point. A class which is conducted on a discussion basis, for example, needs to be small enough for general partici-

[6] Cynthia C. Wedel, "Group Life in the Church," *International Journal of Religious Education*, Vol. 33, No. 9, p. 15. Used by permission.

pation. If it grows to about twenty-five members, it may reach the point where it cannot continue to add members without changing the character of its program. The members may not be conscious of this. They may just unconsciously slacken their efforts to reach others. New members may not be attracted to a group which has reached the upper limit of possibilities for participation.

Groups must grow. If they are to grow as face-to-face personal groups, they must divide to grow. Bringing new groups into existence is often as important as bringing new people into the group. Too often we think that the division of a group is a form of weakness. We make a fetish of numbers.

A prayer fellowship of students at a large university found that their vital Christian experience attracted others, though they made no effort to grow. In fact, so many others were attracted to the group that the members began to lose something of the intense interpersonal relationship which had given their group its character. Deciding that twelve was the maximum number for their purposes, they were not content to be simply a fellowship of twelve persons. They decided that when their group exceeded twelve in number, they would arbitrarily divide into two groups of six or seven. Experience showed that those new groups soon reached the maximum number, and dividing was again necessary. As individuals found acceptance and deep fellowship in the small group, others heard of it and wanted to join.

Opportunities for finding oneself in relationship with others may be a more important outcome of life in the church group than the tasks which the group accomplishes. When the sum of the accomplishments of the smaller, more personal groups is totaled, it is always more than the accomplishment of one large impersonal group.

Group outreach is not fulfilled with the seeking of new members only. It involves the conservation of present membership as well. A truly redemptive group will have a genuine interest in those who are absent and will immediately establish friendly contact with them. When a member does leave the group, it will seek to find the real reason why that person left and will attempt to correct any fault in the group which may cause its members to drop away. What is the point of reaching people if we can't assimilate those we reach? If the members of the group are having many opportunities to participate, if "the way things are done" is "as Christian as the professed purposes of the group,"[7] if the group really exists for something other than itself and its own enjoyment, and if the needs of all persons are truly met, then the new members will be assimilated. Only when it has groups that function in this manner can the church become a living cell in the body of Christ exercising a redeeming influence.

## Questions for Discussion

1. How much of the activity of your church group is really directed by the stated purpose of the group?

2. How can a group work at a specific task and still be person-centered?

3. How is it possible for every group, board, and committee in the church to have a redemptive purpose?

4. What unmet needs could be met and unreached persons reached by the development of new groups in your church?

5. How can church members achieve a high degree of solidarity and yet not withdraw from the world which Christ sends them as witnesses?

## Suggested Reading

*The Group Workshop Way in the Church,* Paul F. Douglass, Association Press, Nashville, 1956.

This author applies group workshop techniques to a wide range of aspects of the church's program.

*Dynamics of Participative Groups,* Jack R. Gibb, Grace N. Platts, and Lorraine F. Miller, Copyright, 1951, by J. R. Gibb.

This practical guide to groups and how they operate was prepared by group dynamics specialists.

*The Church Redemptive,* Howard Grimes, Abingdon Press, Nashville, 1958. Chapters VIII and IX.

*Fellowship Evangelism Through Church Groups,* Harry C. Munro, The Bethany Press, St. Louis, 1951.

Developed out of the fellowship evangelism program of the National Christian Teaching Mission, this book is a local church manual on this type of evangelism.

[7] Cynthia C. Wedel, *ibid.,* p. 15.

# V

# Effective Group Functioning in the Church

We have had frequent occasion, as we have examined the group experience of persons and the group life of the church, to point to the need of effective groups. Some of the characteristics of these groups have been given in various contexts. One of the most important factors determining the character of a group is the group's way of doing things. An inadequate group can be increased in effectiveness by changing its atmosphere and method of operation. An effective personal group can be improved by attention to the group process. For this reason we want to look more closely at group functioning* in the church.

## A. VALUE PLACED UPON PERSONS AND THEIR PARTICIPATION

Groups which are effective in changing lives give attention to persons. We have noted that personhood is basic to the Christian philosophy of life. We have also seen that groups must meet the needs of persons. Some principles which can guide groups in relation to persons and which have been suggested in previous chapters can now be set forth as part of the basis of effective group functioning.

### 1. Each Individual Is Important as a Person

No person was too small, too sinful, too insignificant to be of concern to the Master. He rebuked his disciples for turning away the little children. He dealt mercifully with the woman taken in adultery. He expressed some of the most profound truth to the outcast Samaritan woman at the well.

* FUNCTIONING—executing or performing any duty, office, responsibility, or act.

Human personality, though riven by sin, is made in the image of God and has, through divine grace, capacity for great goodness. Judging as we do by the outward appearance, we often fail to see the potential in each person. But the potential is there and gives value to the individual. It is in relatedness that this capacity can be made real. If our groups are to be effective in developing human capacities, each person must be considered important.

## 2. Each Person Has a Contribution to Make

It must be because we think so well of ourselves and our own abilities, or because we think so ill of others, that most of us overlook the capabilities of others to contribute to our thought and development and to the progress of the group. A father who had been offered a new position in a distant city shared with his family the fact that he was pondering this decision. The small boy of the family looked up and asked, "But, Daddy, do they have schools in that town?" He was due to start school next year and that, to him, was more important than his father's salary, working conditions, abilities, or anything else. The father answered, "Yes, of course they do." But he admitted that his son's question started him thinking on a subject he had heretofore overlooked: the quality of the educational opportunities for his children in the new location.

Every member of the group has some contribution to make and should not only be allowed to make it, but should also be encouraged and helped, if necessary, to do so.

## 3. Each Person Has Something to Gain from Others

Each one of us has the potentialities of personhood. For those potentialities to be realized we need to have relationship with one another. Much as we may gain in terms of material possessions or knowledge from our contacts with others in groups, the most important gains are in relationships and personal development. One cannot develop as a father without a family. One cannot become a leader apart from a group. In fact, one cannot be entirely human alone. Love is the true power that calls persons into being. But we don't love in the abstract. We learn to love and be loved when we develop relationships of depth with others. We may be attracted to a stranger, but we learn to love those with whom we share common memories, experiences, hopes, and ideals. Being accepted, recognized, wanted for one's own sake, needed, and loved — these are the experiences that contribute the most to us as persons.

### 4. Each Person's Contribution to the Group Is Important to Him

We may have to confess that we don't see the relevance of a statement made in a discussion, but we cannot completely ignore or rule out the statement of any individual in the group if we have a real concern for persons. What George says seems relevant to him. To us it may seem to be a sign of his misunderstanding of what the goals of the group are or what the problem is that the group is facing. His comment and behavior may be symptomatic of his own personal problems. They may reveal hostility or insecurity. But to George his words and actions are important, and to squelch or ignore the disturbing remark or behavior may be more serious for the outcome of the group process than spending a moment dealing with an irrelevancy or a hostile remark.

Many groups, especially discussion groups, have found it a good rule in this connection to consider any contribution made in the group as group property once it has been made. This is important for the personhood of the contributor, for then his own personal prestige is not dependent upon the success or failure of the suggestion or the acceptance or rejection of the proposal. It ceases to be "George's idea" which he must defend. It becomes the property of the group to examine and accept, reject, or modify as it will.[1]

## B. APPROPRIATE GROUP SETTING

The setting in which the group meets sets the stage for the type of action the group accomplishes.

### 1. The Physical Arrangement of the Group Needs to Be Conducive to the Type of Activity in Which the Group Will Be Engaged

[1] Herbert A. Thelen, *Dynamics of Groups at Work*, Copyright, 1954, by the University of Chicago, The University of Chicago Press, p. 288.

To be seated in rows of pews all facing one direction is entirely satisfactory for a worshiping congregation in a formal worship service. But this arrangement is not good for a Sunday school class where group discussion and problem solving are goals. The ideal arrangement for the small group where maximum participation of all is desired is the rectangle or circle in which each person is face-to-face with each other person.

A small group in a large room makes us feel like small frogs in a big puddle. A large group crowded into a small room gives little breathing space. Either of these conditions, as well as poor lighting, heating, or ventilation, tend to make members of the group concentrate on their physical discomfort rather than on the goals of the group.

## 2. *Proper Equipment Helps a Group Make Progress*

Tables are a help where members of the group may want to write or draw, examine a document, study the Bible or other books or materials. A chalkboard placed where all can see is useful in a discussion group. Where group goals involve activities other than study and discussion, other equipment may be necessary; such as floor space for a children's division class, camping gear for a scout troop, an organ or piano for a choir, and tools for a work group.

## 3. *Numbers Play an Important Part in Group Participation*

What constitutes a satisfactory size and what is optimum size depends on the nature of the group and its goals. Serious thought ought to be given to the question of how large a local church should be. There can be no doubt that we err in both directions. We have congregations so small that in some cases it is literally true that the minister serves as a private chaplain to a small group of families or even a single family. On the other hand, we have congregations so large that it is impossible for the members to know each other, or even for the full-time employees of the congregation, the minister and his staff, to find out who all the members are.

In most churches there must be smaller groups within the total congregation to provide the personal face-to-face relationships that are so necessary. But even these groups face the problem of size. Groups ought to be small enough for maximum participation.

I never liked volleyball as a game because I learned to play it in a high school gym class where the teacher put half the boys on each side of the net. With fifteen boys on a team, I rarely got a chance to hit the ball and thought the game slow, dull, and uninteresting. A dozen years later I fell in with a group of graduate students in a large university, who played volleyball for recreation. There, with no more than six men on a side and with some practice in teamwork that increased participation, I found the game both interesting and challenging. This is frequently the case with group goals. If there are too many people in the group, not all the powers of all the members can be effectively used. Some persons may be shoved aside or drop out because of sheer boredom.

Tom Allan tells of a striking incident in his attempt to help a young man with a prison record, who was brought into a church group by another man he had known in prison.

"For months we did what we could for him. And then, for a spell, he disappeared. At a group meeting I asked if anyone knew what had become of Alastair. No one did. He was our responsibility, and we had failed. It was evident that the group was too big to maintain the kind of personal concern which we wanted to achieve." [2]

There is also a danger that groups may be too small for goal attainment. Eleven men are needed for a football team, more for substitutes. Small high schools in the Midwest and West, lacking sufficient manpower, shifted their goals and developed "six-man" football, a modification of the older game. Many groups which are limited in size may have to alter their goals to make them attainable.

A group needs to have enough members so that all the skills and breadth of experience necessary for goal attainment are available. A group which wants to sing may not be sufficiently large until it includes an accompanist.

If a group needs to be representative of a larger constituency, this will influence its effective size. A committee of three or even less can plan the class party. A pulpit com-

² Tom Allan, *op. cit.*, p. 75. Used by permission.

mittee, however, needs to be broadly representative of the congregation and will have to be larger.

The effective size of a group will depend upon the nature and purpose of the group; but it ought to be large enough for the attainment of its goals, small enough for maximum participation, and small enough and frequent enough in meeting to enable each participant to "get all the way around" and fill out his relationship with each other person in the group. Sometimes it may be necessary to alternate meetings of a large body with those of smaller, more personal subgroups. This is the idea of the familiar buzz group technique. The wise pattern used by women's groups in the church, alternating Woman's Society meetings with small circle meetings and regularly regrouping the circles to insure broad personal relationships throughout the society, might well be copied by other groups.

## C. PROFICIENCY IN GROUP METHOD

When we talk of group methods, we are not thinking in terms of skills for manipulating people. Quite the contrary; group methods have been developed to enable group members to gain greater freedom for responsible group participation. The principles on which these methods are based are as applicable to church groups as to any others.

### 1. Effective Groups Have Goals Which the Members Know and Share

A group doesn't make satisfactory progress unless it knows what its goals are and is oriented toward them. When a group doesn't know where it is going, it had better stop and find out. Time spent in this way will not be lost, for the process of goal formation can serve to increase the togetherness of the group. The group makes the most progress when it is united in seeking group goals. Its progress is slowed when the members are seeking their own personal goals rather than those of the group. When the group's goals are explicit, because they have been worked out with each member participating, individual involvement in decision making and in "we-feeling" is increased.

Let's take the example of the organized adult Sunday

73

church school class. What are its purposes? Does anyone know? It must be seeking many goals if one is to judge by its activities. On Sunday morning it meets regularly for Bible study. Apparently the imparting of biblical content is a goal. Yet the study of the Bible for its own sake does not seem to be the only goal, for there are occasional attempts to grapple with the deeper issues of life in terms of the biblical faith. Then when the class gathers for its monthly meetings, other purposes become evident. The report of the treasurer and of the ways and means committee on the last dinner served to the Kiwanis Club and on the new curtains for the church parlor makes the "ladies aid" type of goal seem uppermost. When the president wonders how she can get out as many members for the Sunday morning sessions of the class as come for the monthly social, the sociability goal comes into view.

The goals of a church group may be worked out by the group itself, or they may be, and sometimes are, handed down to the group by the church and its leadership. In either case, a church group, since it is the church in action, must ultimately address itself to the goals of the total church. That goal, as we have indicated, is to affirm the lordship of Christ and to seek to live as his subjects in the world. This involves the proclamation of the gospel. The church is called to witness; therefore, church groups, too, must witness to the judgment, redeeming love, and mercy of God. Since the witness is a person-to-person one, it is especially effective in face-to-face groups. All church groups must formulate their goals, therefore, in terms of witnessing to persons. Even task-centered groups must be person-centered, at least in part, if they are to be true to the redemptive purpose of the church.

## 2. Flexibility of Procedure Aids Group Effectiveness

Each group develops its own culture, its own way of doing things. Each group has and develops a set of rules by which it controls its own procedure and its members' participation. Sometimes these are unwritten rules which are simply understood by those who have been members of the group, but which have to be discovered through experience by every newcomer. This may mean that a new participant will not know what to expect when he makes a comment or a suggestion, because he is unfamiliar with the culture of the group.

Sometimes the rules are clearly set forth in a constitution and by-laws. The advantage of their being explicit may be offset by their greater rigidity. Yet, whether written or unwritten, the rules of the group may be quite binding in their effect. The danger is that they may stifle initiative and spontaneity. A group which is to be really dynamic in affecting the lives of people will have to retain considerable flexibility of organization and action.

A church is not an audience to be addressed by a preacher, nor is it an order to be controlled by a rigid discipline. It is a deliberative and decision-making community. As such, it and the groups within it need adaptable but orderly procedure.

Flexibility brings direct benefits to the group. The abilities and interests of people differ. This means that not everyone can participate to the same extent in all activities. Changes in activity of the group result in the need for different abilities and thus bring different people to the fore. When the men's group shifts from planning the service for layman's Sunday to painting the chairs in the kindergarten room, different men make the most significant contributions. The aim is not to achieve equal participation but to deal with problems and organize activities in such a way that everyone who wants to participate can do so within the limits of his abilities.

### 3. Continued Evaluation Fosters Group Progress

Not only does a group need to know where it is going and what its goals are, it also needs to have some measure of progress toward achieving those goals. This calls for a constant evaluation of the program and methods of the group. Many church groups have gone on for years doing things in the same old way without ever asking whether those methods are appropriate to the persons and situations now being faced. Even the language they use ceases to be relevant to the times in which they live. Frequent evaluation helps to keep a group oriented in relation to its goals. It keeps the members aware of those goals and their progress toward them and permits intelligent modification of the group process.

75

Some students of group dynamics advocate that the group consciously observe itself as a group at work, study the inter-personal relations within the group, and judge whether it is moving successfully toward its goals. Others feel that giving too much attention to *how* they do it may keep groups from *doing* it. They might be like the centipede who was asked how he kept his many legs from getting tangled when he walked. The centipede had never thought about it before; but when he thought about where each leg ought to be in relation to each other leg, he tripped all over himself. Too much self-consciousness on the part of the group may thwart the very goals it is seeking to attain.

There are a number of techniques of evaluation open to groups involving various degrees of self-consciousness. A few are suggested here with the warning that too much attention to group process may not be good for the group, but that some attention to it helps most groups. How much is too much will depend on the previous experience and maturity of the group.

The "group process observer" is a person assigned to give his attention to how the group is operating rather than to the goal toward which the group is striving. At the end of a meeting he can help by calling attention to the times when members of the group wandered from the subject and when their own personal goals got in the way of the group goals. He can help some members to see that they are over-partici-pating and are thus inhibiting the participation of others.

But it is not necessary to assign a specific person to this task. The group can do this for itself by taking a few min-utes as the session closes to discuss, "What did we accom-plish today and how did we do it, or why did we fail?" Jack Gibb and his associates suggest the use of a check list of group attitudes and behaviors for all members of the group to use. Samples of these are printed in their book.[3] Some groups have used participation charts successfully, where the number of times and even the amount of time each member of a discussion group participated is recorded and then shown to

[3] Jack R. Gibb, Grace N. Platts, and Lorraine F. Miller, *Dynamics of Participative Groups*, Copyright, 1951, by I. R. Gibb, pp. 46-50.

the group, so that each member can evaluate his own contribution to the group's activity. A less self-conscious device for evaluation, but not always a very productive one, is the analysis of the minutes of the meeting to see what proportion of the group's procedure was directed toward goal attainment. The usefulness of this technique will vary with the type of record kept by the secretary and the secretary's perceptiveness with regard to group process.

### 4. Consensus Is the Basis for Action in Effective Groups

Groups move and persons are changed by consensus and agreement, not by controversy. An emotionally charged discussion is not a good discussion, but many people fail to recognize the difference between argument and debate, on the one hand, and discussion on the other. In the former, the attempt is made to overpower the opposition in one way or another. The goal of the one who argues is to inflict his views upon another. Discussion, on the other hand, is at its best a mutual sharing of information, understandings, and insights in a co-operative effort to solve a problem, reach a decision, or discover the truth.

Through this process it is possible to come to a consensus, a unanimity of purpose which becomes the basis for concerted action. We sing, "Like a mighty army moves the church of God." But often the church doesn't move; and it doesn't move because it fails to get the general agreement which is necessary for action involving the whole group. This failure to reach consensus is the result of failure in the group process. Majority-minority cleavages are allowed to split the group and to destroy wholehearted commitment to a course of action. The pressure for decision — either the pressure of time or the pressure of persons — forces groups to vote before there has been sufficient discussion for agreement to be reached. We call for a vote before people are ready to vote, or in a situation where a vote is not appropriate. The resulting split decision leaves members of the group dissatisfied and feeling that they are outside the decision-making wing of the group. To avoid a split decision, we frequently arrive at a false unanimity. This may result either from failure to consider all sides of the question or from an effort (e.g., use of the motion

77

to make the vote unanimous) to gloss over and not recognize honest differences of opinion.

Many of our troubles in this area stem from the halo we have put around majority rule. The church, the fellowship of the Holy Spirit, should be guided not by what most people want, but by what is right and true and in line with the will of God. The presumption on which we operate democratically in the church is that since the members are committed persons, they will be seeking the will of God, and what is the desire of the majority, therefore, will be his will. Actually, however, each of us seeks to win others to our own point of view. None of us understand the will of God perfectly. And all of us could well use others' ideas as a good basis for checking our own ideas to see if they are founded on self-will or God's will. As Christians we are seeking the truth in love and commitment under the guidance of the Holy Spirit. Democratic procedures are appropriate only when they help us to consider the views and needs of others and thus enable us to approach ever closer to God's will for our lives.

### 5. *Awareness of the Needs and Goals of Others Makes Possible Free and Total Commitment to Action*

Quicker solution of conflict situations comes where the needs and goals of others are considered. There is also less sense of having had to make a sacrifice. The confirmed bachelor may not want to get married because of the freedoms he will have to sacrifice for married life. But look at the young man who has found the right young woman. A great affection has sprung up between them. They have been together enough to know that they share common ideals and goals. When this has happened, the young man doesn't feel that the abandonment of his freedoms is a sacrifice at all. He doesn't have to "give them up." He freely and willingly discards them for the new joint goals he shares with his intended. So it is with the group participant in the church. He is committed to Christ and to the Christian community. He has shared in the shaping of the goals of the group. When there is real consensus in the group about the goals and the way in which they are to be sought, the group goals become his goals. He doesn't have to sacrifice himself for the sake of the church. He gives himself with a fervent faith to the work of the church because it is his work and the work of God.

## D. GOOD INTERPERSONAL RELATIONS

Very important to the effectiveness of groups, their results in decision making or task performance, and their effect upon persons, is the matter of relations among the persons in the group. We often hear: "We got nowhere in the committee because Tom Ross, as usual, talked all the time"; "Deacon Jones was on the one side, so, of course, Mrs. Dever had to be on the other"; "We were having a good discussion until the minister walked in, then everyone clammed up"; "Walter was chairman, and he had it all worked out so that all we had to do was to rubber stamp his plan"; "We followed parliamentary procedure all right. We kept the minutes and wasted the hours." Each of these comments suggests a way in which interpersonal relations can affect group progress. The following paragraphs describe some of the steps that can be taken to improve interpersonal relations in church groups.

### 1. Friendly Informality Aids Group Performance

Discussion or action groups find that informality is a must. If people in the group are not already acquainted, they need time to get acquainted. Presumably the members of a class or a youth fellowship know each other, at least on a superficial basis, but even though they do, introductions of new people are often needed. In conferences and conventions, where people who do not know each other are thrust together, a more extended time of getting acquainted may be helpful. Don't save all the "socializing" for the end of the meeting. Try putting the coffee break first. There is a danger here, however. Too much informality may lead to triviality, and that, too, may keep the group from getting anywhere.

Titles and ranks are out of place in a group which seeks real togetherness. Persons need to participate in a group on their own merit as persons, not on the basis of previous attainments and honors. One who is spoken of as "Reverend" or "Doctor" may constitute a serious block to the participation of others. Get the group on a "first name basis." The demand for the recognition of titles may show a personal insecurity on the part of the individual making the demand.

Even where, by their very nature, some aspects of the group's activity must be formal (e.g., a plenary session of a large group or the formal worship services of a church) the advantages of informality may not be entirely lost. The worshipers in a country church often stand around in the vestibule or outdoors engaging in friendly conversation until time for the service to start. Some new churches are being constructed with the entrance to the sanctuary leading through a large social room or parlor to encourage the members to know each other personally. A number of large city churches use a coffee hour after the morning service so that worshipers may have opportunity to meet each other and share experiences and ideas with one another and with their pastor.

## 2. Pleasant Interpersonal Relationships Improve Group Functioning

Strained emotional relationships among people are the real barriers to effective social action. When people feel uncertainty, discomfort, or fear in the presence of others, they hold back in their participation, or they participate in ways that do not represent their real selves. In a small church where the trustees had failed to do their job, the pastor talked with several church members in their homes and in small groups about the need for electing a responsible board of trustees. He got complete agreement. But when the annual business meeting came along and one of the trustees was nominated for re-election, no one rose in the meeting to nominate anyone else, and no one voted against the inactive, incumbent trustee. They didn't dare oppose him.

"We may for many reasons feel uncomfortable or hostile (feel 'threat') in the presence of other people. The reasons may not be at all clear to the persons involved. Situations and people may remind us of people and situations we have experienced in the past. Also, people and situations wholly new to us may make us uncomfortable. The fear and underlying hostilities which result will affect our reactions in the group and cause tensions to arise. The group members may have jealousies, fears, or frustrations of which they are unaware. These may cause tension that prevents complete orientation toward problem-solving. Many activities of the group that are apparently problem-oriented are often simply subconscious attempts to solve these interpersonal conflicts."[4]

Pleasant interpersonal relations are clearly important in reducing this sort of obstacle to group effectiveness. A group in which the members know each other, enjoy each other's company, and are sincerely interested in each other as persons is a group most likely to gain full and effective participation. In a group where the relations between people are not pleasant, the tendency is to shift attention from group goals to interpersonal goals. We become more interested in defeating the argument of another than in getting at the truth. We become more concerned about developing an activity in which we can excel than in doing what is best for the group. Even nominating someone for an office may be an expression of hostility. It may be an attempt to load work upon an unsuspecting or already overworked member as a sort of revenge for previous experiences.

Heated discussion is not good discussion. It brings emotion to bear on the problem, rather than thought. Emotional outbursts and problem persons are group problems because they stir up unpleasant interpersonal feelings which thwart group progress. Interpersonal problems often have to be solved before group problems can be faced.

## 3. Depth of Interpersonal Penetration Is Essential to Effective Group Functioning

The atmosphere of the church group must not be that of skimming the surface. We deal with the deepest and most basic understandings of human life. But much of the world gets the impression that the church and church people do not penetrate to the depths of reality. We discuss fine points of doctrine and biblical exegesis. We drift into the use of pious platitudes. We involve only a minimum of ourselves in our relations with others, when our total being ought to be involved. No trivialities entered the conversation of the men

[4] Gibb, Platts, and Miller, *ibid.*, p. 7. Used by permission.

who were trapped hundreds of feet below the surface of the earth in the Spring Hill, Nova Scotia, mine disaster. In the depths of the earth, out of communication with the men on the surface, and not knowing if they would ever get out, they earnestly discussed every avenue of escape. Every query was an exploration of previous experience and the present situation for possibilities of being saved. Every opinion shared related to this one essential question. We who see the disaster of a world trapped in the depths, out of communication with the God who is its salvation, if men but knew it, must not just pass the time and fritter away our energies with the routine and trivial. We must deal with matters of real significance.

"The development of a kind of togetherness in which men and women rediscover the reality of fellowship at a deep level is one of the really good things of our generation, and one which has possibilities for the future beyond what we can now envisage."[5]

## 4. Church Groups Function Best in an Atmosphere of Democracy, Frankness, and Love

We all give lip service to democracy, but our practice of it, both in and out of the church, falls far short of our profession. Democracy is not always easy to practice. Sometimes our personal ambitions get in the way. At other times we may withdraw from participation, or become boldly aggressive and run rough-shod over others, because of personal feelings of insecurity, fear, and uncertainty. Our behavior is often an effort to cover up these feelings and conceal them, even from ourselves. Afterward we wonder what "devil" got into us to make us behave as we did.

Another part of our difficulty in practicing democracy lies in our unthinking acceptance of certain common clichés. We hear and say, "There are two sides to every question." With this idea as our basis we try to deal with all questions in terms of votes for or against a motion, and we respond to all persons as though they were for or against a proposal. Often there are as many sides to a question as there are participants in the group. Instead of forcing people to line up on sides, we need to share ideas in a permissive atmosphere until the

[5] D. Elton Trueblood, *op. cit.*, p. 14. Used by permission.

group comes to some consensus or agreement. After that a vote on the motion may be a mere formality. General agreement has already been reached in a meeting of minds. The premature proposing of a motion and the early call for a vote on the question may be among the most undemocratic of procedures, even though negative votes are tolerated.

Another cliché thwarting democracy is that "discussion is simply the pooling of ignorance." To be democratic is not to be blind or uninformed. It is quite within the realm of democratic procedure to conduct whatever research is necessary to get the needed facts. Facts are not a matter of discussion. They simply are, and must be recognized. It is only the interpretation of facts that is open to discussion. But many groups waste time and human resources of energy discussing matters that simple reference to sources of fact could settle. If the facts needed are not immediately available, the meeting had better be postponed until the facts can be assembled. However, facts are not always easy to adjust to, and they do not interpret themselves. People need to "try them on for size," look at them from all angles, and come to what is for them a satisfactory relationship to those facts. These are among the functions of discussion.

The democracy of group participation is based on the Christian philosophy we have already outlined, the philosophy of personhood. Each person is important in his own right. He has a right to an opinion and an expression of it. His opinion and his contribution to the group have value even though they may be rejected when the group finally makes its decision. The very fact of participation and expression of a point of view is of value to the individual participating, to other members of the group as individuals, and to the group as a whole.

This sort of democracy is not achieved unless there is freedom both from domination and submission. Squelching ignores the value of the person. The steam roller that flattens opposition and the bulldozer that shoves other points of view out of the way are both out of place in the church group.

In the Christian group frankness is a must. Flattery and fawning are basically dishonest and have no place. Real sharing and the direct personal exchange which are so important to the spreading of the gospel are not achieved unless people are honest with each other. Most of us tend to be brutally frank when discussing the shortcomings of others and somewhat less than honest about ourselves. Sometimes we cannot be honest because we do not adequately understand ourselves. At this point the group is an aid, for as we participate more freely and develop a closeness to one another, self-deception becomes more difficult, and we begin to understand ourselves and our reactions as never before.

Underlying all other elements in the atmosphere of the redemptive group is self-forgetting love. Christians speak the truth in love. They are governed by love not only because it is a good way for persons to behave in groups, but also because, having experienced the love of God in Christ and having denied self, there is no other acceptable way to live. As Christians we love each individual as a free person, not seeking to bind him to ourselves or use him. Christian love seeks to share and to serve. It does not seek to move others so much as to be moved by sharing the experience of others. Love is always expressed in relationships, in *koinonia*, the real fellowship of the Spirit.

> "Blest be the tie that binds
> Our hearts in Christian love;
> The fellowship of kindred minds
> Is like to that above."

## Questions for Discussion

1. Why do tensions between persons get in the way even when the group members are Christians?

2. How can we eliminate the feeling of insecurity and the feeling of being in some way threatened that keep people from free and active sharing in our groups?

3. How can majority rule interfere with Christian fellowship and with the guidance of the Holy Spirit?

4. Why is informality needed for a group to be creative and effective?

5. How does Christian love change the effect of democracy and frankness in the group?

## Suggested Reading

*How to Work with Church Groups,* Mary Alice Douty, Abingdon Press, Nashville, 1957.

Principles of group work for leaders of groups in the church are set forth in this book.

*You Can't Be Human Alone,* Margaret E. Kuhn, The Judson Press, Philadelphia, 1956.

This leadership training course emphasizes the role of face-to-face groups in the development of human personality.

*Learning Together in the Christian Fellowship,* Sara Little, John Knox Press, Richmond, 1956.

Group methods are effectively applied to Christian education.

*The Group Workshop Way in the Church,* Paul F. Douglass, Association Press, Nashville, 1956.

*Group Dynamics in Evangelism,* Paul M. Miller, Herald Press, Scottdale, Pa., 1958.

# VI

# Leadership, Communication, and the Christian Fellowship

## A. CHRISTIAN GROUP LEADERSHIP

Leadership is needed in any organization. Just how important we consider it to be to the groups in which we take part is indicated by the remarks we often make or hear: "We failed because of poor leadership"; "A group can rise no higher than its leadership"; "The trouble with the organization is that it has no leadership"; "First Church has an abundance of leadership"; "Just when things looked darkest, a leader arose and saved the day." We also recall Jesus' comments on the dangers of not being well led: "He had compassion on them, because they were like sheep without a shepherd" (Mark 6:34) and "Can a blind man lead a blind man? Will they not both fall into a pit?" (Luke 6:39).

We all agree that we need it, but we are not always sure what leadership is; and frequently we are at a loss to know where to turn for it. Sometimes it seems to us that situations call forth leaders. We have seen persons who were not previously recognized as leaders rise to great heights under the pressure of a crisis situation. At other times we feel that leaders make situations. The presence of a person of recognized ability seems to shape the course of events so that his or her ability finds expression in and puts its stamp upon those events.

## 1. Leadership Is a Social Role

Situations do develop leaders, and leaders do change situations. Leadership is built upon a complex of abilities and traits in the individual; but it is also dependent upon specific situations. This is what complicates the problem of obtaining leadership. If leadership consisted of abilities and traits alone, we would have no difficulty finding it. We could identify the needed traits, find the people who have them, and know immediately who our leaders should be. In all situations, the persons having the necessary leadership traits would be our leaders.

But the situation is not so simple as this. There are no "leaders" as such. Leadership is more specific and is related to the activities of the group. One who is a leader in one activity may not be in another. Vernon may be a leader in the educational program of the church, but not in the financial. Dorothy may be able to organize and direct the choir, but she is not necessarily the one who can best head the committee to frame the new church constitution.

Just as there are no "leaders" as such, there is no "leadership" in isolation. Leadership is a social role, a group function. It is an interaction process between the group and certain members of the group who take on some specialized functions for the group. This means that regardless of his abilities and traits, an individual's rise to leadership is dependent on the group's goals, the situation of the group, and the capacity of the individual to contribute to the attainment of those goals in that particular situation.

Members of a pulpit committee recognize this in seeking a new pastor for the church. They know that by virtue of his formal position the new pastor will be a leader in several aspects of the church program. What aspects will depend on the church's goals and its situation. The committee, therefore, will have to be more than a good judge of men to pick out the one who can best lead the congregation. It will also have to have a clear knowledge of the goals of the church and of the group culture, that is, the church's way of doing things. In addition, it will have to be thoroughly conversant with the situation of the church, both in terms of the needs and problems of its own organization and the needs and problems of the surrounding community. Only then will the pulpit committee know what sort of leadership to seek.

The ability of the leader to contribute to the attainment of group goals cannot always be measured in terms of his own technical skill. The best player on the team does not always make the best captain. The largest contributor may not be the best chairman for a financial campaign. The leader may make his chief contribution to the attainment of group goals through his capacity to stimulate and co-ordinate the efforts of others. Like the coach or team captain, a pastor or a church group leader will find his main tasks to be these: to kindle interest and enthusiasm; to train, aid, and inspire; to seek out the special talent of each member; to maintain order and efficiency for the good of the group; to suppress his own ego and encourage the progress of those he leads. Capacity for these tasks is not so easy to recognize as technical skill, but it is more important to the success of the group.

## 2. Group Leadership Demands Special Qualities

Leadership is built, we have said, on a complex of abilities and traits. A questioner might ask: What are the distinctive attributes of leaders? Many lists of these attributes have been made, and no two of them are exactly alike. It is not our purpose here to make a new list, nor to combine all other lists of leadership traits into one exhaustive list. There are, however, some traits that are particularly appropriate in face-to-face personal groups. These we will examine briefly.

Naturally, *technical competence* in the field of the group's interest is important. One does not choose as an adult Sunday church school class teacher someone who does not know how to teach, or someone who knows little about the Bible.

Groups need leadership with *initiative*. Leaders need to be able to think and act without being urged. Groups tend to be slow to start and to wander aimlessly at times. Someone who will assume responsibility for taking the first move, who will begin action, fulfills an important group function.

Related to initiative in the progress of the group is the need for someone who is able to *explore* and to be *creative*. Group leaders need to have the ability to originate new ideas and encourage others to do so. Many competent members of a group just do not qualify for filling this role.

Groups also need someone who is a *gate keeper** and *expediter.*** The irrelevant needs to be kept out. Facilitating

* GATE KEEPER—a member of a group who is alert to the fact that certain members of the group are not participating in the group's immediate concern, and accordingly tries to involve them.
** EXPEDITER—one who keeps the group moving toward its desired goal.

the concentration of the energy of the group upon the problem at hand is a valuable service toward group goal attainment.

A group leader needs to have *insight* and *foresight*. He will need to steer the group in light of the consequences of its action. If he is to do this, he will need to be able to anticipate the consequences of certain types of behavior in the group or of a proposed course of action. He must consider the consequences not just for the group as a whole and for the goals it seeks, but also for persons, both in and out of the group.

*Empathy** and *communication* are also key characteristics of group leadership. The leader needs to be able to feel with the group. It is good if he can understand and even anticipate the members' reactions. He needs also to be able to share with them his insights and his ideas. This he cannot do unless he is able to communicate.

A sense of *timing* is valuable, too, since timing plays such an important part in the success or failure of ideas and enterprises.

Because leadership is a social role, the characteristics we have mentioned here are those which have the most direct bearing upon group activity. Even a definition of leadership must be in terms of group experience. One of the simplest and best is given us by Herbert Thelen:

> "Leadership is the set of functions through which the group co-ordinates the efforts of individuals. These efforts must result in satisfaction to the participants, as well as in help to the group in meeting its purposes."[1]

The emphasis in this definition and in our discussion is on the function of leadership rather than on the person who performs the function. Leadership is the process of mutual stimulation which controls and directs the application of the abilities and energies of the group in pursuit of the group goals.

### 3. Church Groups Have Both Formal and Dynamic Leaders

Some persons carry out the functions of leadership because they are in positions where these functions are expected of

---

* EMPATHY—the ability of a leader or member of a group to identify himself with the other members of the group and to feel their needs and concerns.

[1] Herbert A. Thelen, *op. cit.*, p. 296. Used by permission.

them. These have been called the *formal leaders*. The pastor is the formal leader of a local church. Whether called or assigned, once on the field, he is in a position of religious leadership and will be expected to fill different leadership roles in a variety of situations. The teacher of a children's class or the assigned counselor or sponsor of a youth group is in a formal position of leadership, responsible for guiding children and youth in their Christian education. Elected officers, once they are chosen, accede to positions of formal leadership. In most organizations we do not choose a new chairman for each meeting in terms of the needs of the group at that time. We depend on the president or moderator to carry out the leadership functions because he is already in a position of formal leadership.

These formal leaders are important because they give continuity in the carrying out of group functions. However, they are not always the most effective leaders. There may be little or no relation between the attaining of the positions they hold and the felt needs of the group, which call forth the leadership function. An extreme case would be the hereditary monarch, leader of a nation by the accident of birth. Almost as extreme from the point of view of the group is the person from the outside designated as the leader of a children's or youth group. He will need every support he can get, including a successful attempt to identify himself with the group he leads. Even if a person has been elected to a leadership position, the circumstances and goals of the group may have changed, or his relationship with the group may have changed so that he no longer represents the real feeling and need of the group.

If the gap between the group and its formal leadership is great, the work of another kind of leader is important. This is the *dynamic leader*, the one who has influence in the group because the others watch him for his reactions, take their cues from him, and count on him for the initiation of group action. This person does not always appear in a position of formal leadership. But he is the one who gets things done in the group, regardless of position. Some would call this "natural leadership." It is not "natural" in the sense of being an inherent quality, but it is natural in the sense of arising out of the group situation. We might also call this "chosen leadership" because it is called into being by the group. A dynamic leader may have qualities that fit a particular situation, he may have become symbolic of group goals, or he may be looked to by the group for leadership out of habit.

It is important to work with dynamic leaders because they are in touch with the full life of the group. Often they have contact with group members outside the regular meeting times of the group and can continue to further the goals of the group even when it is not assembled. Informal groups assign leadership responsibility to dynamic leaders freely and "naturally." Organizations with more formal structures need to develop sufficient flexibility so that dynamic leaders can be used, whether they hold formal positions or not. Assigned leaders from outside the group need to discover, know, and work through dynamic leaders in order to foster group progress and to keep leadership where it belongs, in the group.

## 4. Democracy Is Strengthened by the Distribution of Leadership Roles

We customarily think of leaders as being either democratic or autocratic. Actually, these are two extreme types, and there are many variations in between. The difference between the extremes was vividly demonstrated by the social psychologists Lewin and Lippitt in their classic study of groups of children at the University of Iowa. They watched two carefully matched and equal groups of children of the same age working on a project of mask making. One group operated on a democratic basis with the adult leaders giving the children freedom in choice of materials, choice of subjects, and choice of work partners. The second group met two days later with the adult leaders directing the children on an authoritarian basis to do exactly what the children of the other group had freely chosen to do. The behavior of the children was carefully tabulated, and the results showed that the children of the first group not only worked together better but also had a great togetherness as evidenced by the frequent use of "we-centered" statements. The members of the autocratic group made more "I-centered" statements. They were more submissive to the adult leaders, but not to each other. They

Progressing from individual responsibility

1. Leader decides, announces his decision to the group.
2. Leader decides, "sells" his decision to the group.
4. Leader presents tentative decision, subject to change.
5. Leader presents the problem, asks advice, makes decision.

# IN MAKING DECISIONS

(autonomy) to group responsibility

3. Leader presents ideas, invites questions. Decides.
6. Leader defines limits, group decides.
7. Group defines limits, group decides.

expressed a great deal more hostility and even drove two children (whom Lewin called "scapegoats") out of their group.

The leadership of the groups in which we work will probably not be at either extreme but will fluctuate between them as indicated by the diagram on the next two pages. Persons in positions of leadership can, by studying this diagram, discover if their actions tend more in the direction of individual responsibility where the leader does the thinking for the group, or group responsibility where the group does its own thinking. How much responsibility can be shifted to the group will depend on the training and experience the members of the group have in shouldering such responsibility.

When we understand leadership as a set of functions to be performed for the group, we cease to think of one special person as the leader. We discover that leadership functions, such as the stating of problems, maintaining motivation, organizing group goal-seeking, and evaluating group activities, can be spread around among the members of the group. This has been called "participative" or "distributive" leadership.[2] The members of the group need to be trained for this kind of functioning, and it may be that the best leader of the group will be the one who makes himself most dispensable by training others for leadership tasks and distributing these tasks among them. There are groups who function without a leader, as such, because each member has come to feel a sense of responsibility for the group and has been trained to think of ideas and suggestions which we usually expect to come only from the mind of a leader.

Maximum group responsibility is particularly appropriate for the church group. The experience of carrying leadership functions aids in the development of a person to his highest potentialities and is in line with the Christian emphasis upon persons. If we really believe that the Holy Spirit is given to and guides the committed group and not just a few favored individuals, then distributing leadership responsibilities very broadly will give more opportunity for the guidance of the Spirit to be known and felt.

Spreading leadership functions among members of the

[2] Gibb, Platts, and Miller, *op. cit.*, p. 20.

group may also avoid the ego inflation* which is always a danger for "the leader." If this is done, a leader will not seek leadership roles for himself. Instead, he will encourage others to take what responsibility they can. He, himself, will take on responsibilities only in order to serve the group. In this way, he will follow the teaching of Jesus that the leader is not the master of the group but its servant. "I am among you as one who serves" (Luke 22:27). "Whoever would be great among you must be your servant" (Matt. 20:26).

## 5. Christian Groups Need Committed Leadership

The church as the people of God, the body of Christ, the fellowship of the Holy Spirit is made up of committed persons. Yet, as we have seen, some of the members of a local church group may have simply joined an organization rather than a committed fellowship. This means that there is a possibility that the leadership of a local church or a personal group within a church may come into the hands of uncommitted persons. Such persons could not really understand the redemptive purpose of the church and would not lead the group in the direction of its God-given goals. They might seek democracy and broad group participation, but they would not seek the guidance of the Holy Spirit.

Concern for the group, not just as a group, but as a part of the body of Christ with a mission to fulfill in relation to human redemption, should be characteristic of Christian group leaders. Such leaders foster a religious quality in the group, leading the members into an awareness of Christian values both in the definition of group goals and in the interaction of persons in the group.

We are not proposing an inquisition to determine who are committed persons in each group. We should simply remind ourselves that Jesus said, "By their fruits you shall know them." One of his early followers added the test of depth of concern. "We know that we have passed out of death into life, because we love the brethren" (1 John 3:14). "By this we know that we abide in him and he in us, because he has given us of his own Spirt" (1 John 4:13).

* **EGO INFLATION**—when one has a puffed-up idea of himself.

95

## B. COMMUNICATION

Communication is essential to group relations. This might go without saying except that communication problems continue to plague our groups and need attention.

### 1. Language Is a Problem in Communication

It would be impossible to have an effective group if people didn't speak the same language. Yet in most groups we see people who do not understand each other and talk past each other as though they were speaking foreign languages. They say, "You know what I mean," when others haven't the slightest notion of what they are saying. They say, "I hope I have made myself clear," when their hearers are more confused than before they had spoken.

Most of us need more study of language and training in expressing ourselves. With mass communication, twentieth-century man is "more a receptor than a communicator." [3] Instead of getting more experience in expressing our ideas, feelings, and values, we get less.

A detailed discussion of effective language use will be found elsewhere. Here we can only present a few simple rules which may help improve communication in personal groups. First, *use simple, concrete, accurate language.* Don't use a big word when a small one will do. Avoid abstractions and keep your comments close to the experience of those to whom you are talking. Second, *clearness of conception makes for coherence of speech.* If your idea is a bit fuzzy, you may have difficulty imparting it to others. Third, *be sure your hearers understand your definitions of the terms you use.* Such a simple word as "evening" may mean late afternoon to one and anytime before midnight to another. Some groups find it wise, whenever a word is used that might cause confusion, to call a halt for definition of terms. Defining, fact finding, and evaluating are different steps in the group process and mixing them will only lead to confusion. Fourth, *avoid pitfalls of logic.* A single instance doesn't make a general rule. The fact that one event happened before another doesn't mean that the first caused the second.

Language and group experience nurture each other. Lan-

[3] Harvey G. Cox, "Biblical Evangelism in the Twentieth Century," *Foundations*, Vol. II, No. 2, p. 105.

guage grows out of the experience of human groups. Continued interpersonal experience in the group makes communication easier. When I am talking to people with whom I have associated face-to-face for a considerable length of time, I don't have to explain who I am and the background out of which I say what I do. I am already known. And if the associations in that group have penetrated beyond the surface to a real depth level of sharing, I am known more than just by name and background. I am known as the sort of person I really am.

## 2. Emotion Is a Problem in Communication

Even more serious than language as an obstacle to effective group communication are emotional barriers. People cannot be taught if they think that they are somehow being threatened. Group members cannot share their real feelings and opinions when they fear that they will be ridiculed, laughed at, or ignored. People who feel insecure hold tenaciously to pet ideas, wander off into long descriptions of personal experiences, bring up obscure points, resent criticism or suggestions, and generally fail to be good participants. But emotion also plays a role with the one who hears as well as the one who speaks. People respond more to the personality of the speaker than to the ideas he expresses. They hear only what they want to hear. Often they don't understand because deep within themselves they don't want to understand.

It is for this reason that we stressed in Chapter V the importance of good interpersonal relations and group atmosphere. In addition to what is said there, we might point out the special dangers and strengths of Christian personal groups in this field.

All religious experience has a strong emotional quality, and anything connected with religion tends to arouse emotion. Keenly aware of their own past wrongdoings and extremely sensitive to behavior deemed contrary to the will of God, some Christians have given themselves to prophetic denunciations and public chastisement of sins and sinners. This makes a church group a very "threatening" place for one who is aware of his own faults.

It should not be threatening. The Christian, more than

anyone else, should be aware that he himself has been and is a sinner, but for the grace of God. He cannot be self-righteous and be true to his faith that righteousness is a gift of God. Where but in a group of redeemed sinners should a sinner find warm acceptance and sympathetic understanding? As their Master said to the woman caught in adultery, so Christians might say, "Neither do I condemn you" (John 8:11). Christian love and forgiveness improve the atmosphere of acceptance in the group, facilitating communication. Ultimately, they build the togetherness of the Christian community.

## C. DYNAMIC CHRISTIAN FELLOWSHIP

In all our discussion of what we can do to improve the group life of the church through broader participation, shared leadership, and improved communication, we must not forget that Christian fellowship is not something we *do*, but something we *have*. With all our fellowship halls, fellowship hours, and fellowship suppers, we may get to thinking that fellowship is a program item, or something that needs to be worked up, as enthusiasm is aroused by a cheerleader. To avoid this misconception, one is tempted to use the New Testament word *koinonia* in spite of what has been said about language and communication.

Christian fellowship (*koinonia*) exists as a gift of God. It is because the same God has spoken to them all and speaks to them together through his Spirit that Christians have this togetherness. If there is no sense of God's presence and his leadership in the group, there is no *koinonia*, no blessed "tie that binds our hearts in Christian love." The fellowship of the redeemed does not exist apart from God's redemption.

Nevertheless, the feeling of togetherness grows with contact and understanding. Social psychologists point out that frequent interaction on a basis of equality (not of superior with inferior) builds sentiments of liking each other.[4]

"Truest empathy comes not so much from imaginative projection or from similar experiences. It most surely

[4] George C. Homans, *op. cit.*, p. 444.

comes when we have actually participated in shared experiences."[5]

The Christian is, in his redemption, a part of the fellowship. He grows in grace and in the knowledge of Christ as he shares the experiences of the Christian group.

"As God's Word is studied together; as with one another little groups kneel in prayer, confessing their sins and asking for God's mercy and love; as his will asserts dominion over all — they discover a unity because they are fellow children of God, fellow sinners, fellow saints, and joint heirs with Christ in the glories of the kingdom. In such a fellowship is found the sustaining and renewing source of true spiritual community in which there is no East or West, in which the spirit of Christian equality, love, and mutual aid is expressed and, if need be, the barriers of poverty and cultural differences are overcome."[6]

The lone Christian is a person, too, but he did not come into being alone. He became a Christian through the witness of the church, and he will be a more complete and a better Christian in fellowship with a group of Christians. He seeks community because God created him for community. He seeks relationships that will make up for deficiencies in relationships he has already known. He seeks mutual sharing because he wants to be strengthened, and he knows that persons affect and are affected by others. In the group he experiences the corrective, redemptive, and recreative power of the Holy Spirit which flows into the Christian community.

The church and its groups must be dynamic Christian fellowships. They must make use of all that is known about human groups and is in accord with the Spirit of God. In carrying out its redemptive purpose the church group must provide a maximum amount of interpersonal relationship, and this must be at a depth level of sharing of faith and experience. At the heart of the group must be a growing nucleus of concerned persons. Discussion, decision, and action must be carried on in an atmosphere of Christian love. Unless the members are gathered by God and sense the Holy Spirit at work in their midst, they are not a church or a church group.

[5] Daniel J. Fleming, *Living as Comrades*, Agricultural Missions, 1950, p. 8. Used by permission.
[6] Daniel J. Fleming, *ibid.*, p. 18. Used by permission.

There must be in the group the recognition of the presence of God.

When all this becomes true of the church, the church will not be just another group in the community, not just another organization in a highly organized society, but the beloved community, the holy fellowship, the much-to-be-desired home of all redeemed men. Then it will take precedence in our lives not from obligation or duty, but from the experience of the reality of the presence of God, from the joy of our salvation, from the free and wholehearted commitment to be his people and his witnesses in the world. Then the feeling of belonging to the church will be so deeply satisfying in all our lives that no other group could possibly take its place.

Such a church cannot be self-centered. The members cannot think of themselves as gathered for their own sake or for the sake of the fellowship. Its center will be the purpose of God. Its members will know that they are gathered to be dispersed, called that they may be sent out, knit together that they may know their oneness with those who do not know and that they may be messengers of the gospel of redemption to them.

## Questions for Discussion

1. What is a good leader of a church group like?

2. How can a leader encourage the growth of leadership potential in the group?

3. What are some of the emotional barriers to effective sharing in your church?

4. How can the church avoid the criticism that it does not express its faith in language the world of today can understand?

5. What are some of the barriers to communications between the church and the world?

6. How can you help to make your church more redemptive than it is?

## Suggested Reading

*Living as Comrades,* Daniel Johnson Fleming, Agricultural Missions, New York, 1950.

*Dynamics of Groups at Work,* Herbert A. Thelen, University of Chicago Press, Chicago, 1954.

This book contains especially good discussions of shared leadership functions and of problem solving through personal groups.

*How to Develop Better Leaders,* Malcomb S. and Hulda Knowles, Association Press, New York, 1955.

This is a handbook of practical ways to develop and encourage new leadership.